Longman

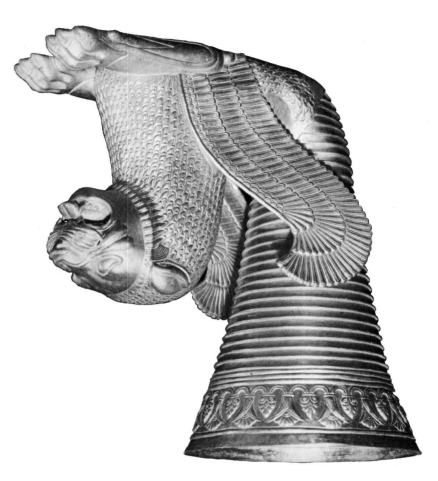

ATLAS
of the
ANCIENT
WORLD

Editorial

Consultant Editor
Amélie Kuhrt

Authors
Christopher Fagg
Frances Halton

Editor
Frances M. Clapham

Assistant Editor
Elizabeth Wiltshire

Top: Fields near Hattusa in Anatolia. Centre: Greek-influenced Indian goldwork (1st or 2nd century AD). Bottom: A village in Egypt in about 3000 BC.

LONGMAN GROUP LIMITED
London

Associated companies, branches and representatives throughout the world

First published 1979

Designed and produced by Grisewood & Dempsey Ltd, Grosvenor House, 141–143 Drury Lane, London W.1.

© Grisewood & Dempsey Ltd, 1979

Printed and bound by Vallardi Industrie Grafiche, Milan, Italy

BRITISH LIBRARY CATALOGUING IN PUBLICATION DATA

Fagg, Christopher
    Atlas of the ancient world.
    1. History, Ancient – Maps
    I. Title
    911'.3   G1033

ISBN 0–582–39042–7

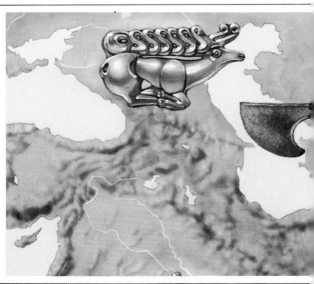

Contents

Top: Cave-paintings at Lascaux (16,000–10,000 BC). Centre: A North Syrian carving (10th or 9th century BC). Bottom: A Chinese hunt (2nd century BC).

Looking at the Past

The way in which people live has always been influenced by the sort of country they live in: by the climate, the crops they can grow, and the animals they can rear; by the building materials and the ease of getting from place to place. Looking at the history of the world by regions, instead of by periods of time, helps us to understand the sort of places in which ancient people lived and how these influenced their civilizations.

Hunting and Farming

The first men fed themselves on seeds and fruit, and by hunting. They moved about, often following herds of animals and going to places where they knew food would be plentiful. They lived in caves, or built themselves very simple huts or tents of branches and skins. Some parts of the world were particularly suitable for this way of life and the people there carried on in the same way for thousands of years.

We can learn a great deal about the past from objects dug up at places where people lived long ago. These places are usually known as 'sites'. They must be very carefully dug so that the exact place where each object is found can be noted down. The picture on the left shows part of a site where a 'dig' is going on. Finds are placed in the labelled boxes; all the earth is taken away to be sieved in case any small find has been missed. The grid of string helps to map the site at different stages.

This picture of dogs hunting a wild boar has been reconstructed from a wall painting at Tiryns in Greece. The darker parts are the original fragments, found in the position in which they are shown here. The artist who painted in the rest has followed what he thought was on the original, from studying similar paintings. These reconstructions are a great help in imagining what ancient places looked like, but sometimes dreadful mistakes are made. An artist doing a reconstruction at Knossos in Crete filled in the figure of a boy picking crocuses. Later researchers decided that the picture showed not a boy, but a monkey!

But in other places, perhaps where the climate was different and food was not so easy to get, people learned to domesticate animals like goats and sheep, cattle and pigs. Instead of harvesting wild grain crops they planted their own, and they developed plants which gave more and better grain.

This kind of life is very hard and needs a lot of continuous work, so men had to stop moving around and build settled homes. They started to adapt the country around them to suit their needs. They cleared the land to make fields for their crops, and they cut down trees for fires and to build houses. They dug water channels to irrigate their crops and turned land that was semi-desert into good farming land. Once all Europe was covered with thick forests, where today there are open fields. Round the Mediterranean coast forests were cut down and olive trees planted. But their deep roots did not hold the top-soil together and it was blown away by the wind and washed away by the rain. People have not always improved the land.

Sites and Trade

When people became dependent on the food they grew, it became important for them to live in places which they could easily defend and which provided the things they needed. These included not only grazing ground, reasonable soil, and enough water but also, as the settlements grew, access to essential materials for building and for making tools. Some, like the Greeks, liked to centre their settlements on a hill which they could fortify. The ancient Chinese built their towns and cities beside rivers, which not only provided water for the crops but also defended them from at least one side. The rivers were also a good way of travelling and of carrying goods. Many important cities grew up because they were on trade routes.

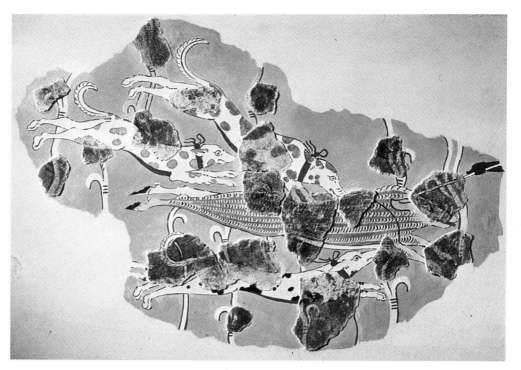

Discovering the Past

We can learn a great deal about the past from the remains of ancient peoples and the things they made, and by studying their written records. But the distant past is like a vast jigsaw puzzle with most of the pieces lost. Although archaeologists have discovered and studied large numbers of fascinating sites there must be many, many others still unknown to us which would help to fill in the picture. Every few years we read of discoveries which teach us a piece of the 'puzzle' has been put into the wrong place and that our previous ideas were quite wrong. This is one reason why new history books sometimes disagree with other, earlier books.

The written records of the past are very valuable; but they do not always tell the true story of what actually happened. For every country tends to write records which show it coming out top – in skills, in learning, in wealth, and in war. In the 14th century BC the pharaoh Ramesses II described how he was cut off from his army by the Hittites, saying he rode at the gallop and charged the enemies, having no one with him: 'I found that 2500 enemy chariots in whose midst I had been lying were broken in pieces before my steeds.' His account does not mention that he had a division of soldiers with him, and that it was his own fault that they were cut off. The Hittites recorded this battle as a draw!

In Roman times we read of good emperors who worked wisely with the Senate, and bad ones who ruled without it; but were these records perhaps written from the Senate's point of view? This is the sort of thing which historians must always remember when they are trying to find out what really happened.

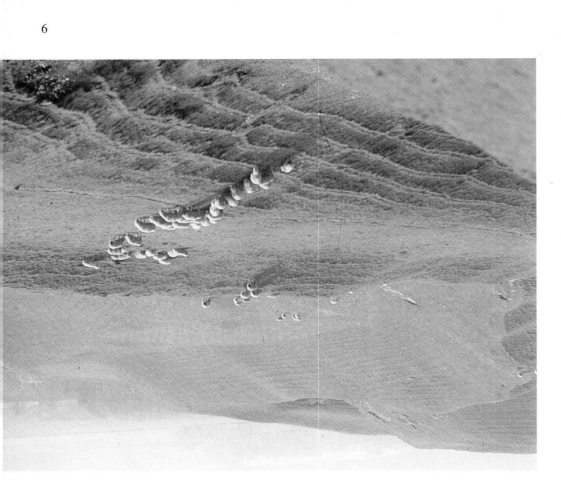

However hard they try to be objective, historians always see the past from the point of view of their own times. If we look at pictures of the past drawn by 19th century artists, we can tell almost at once that they were painted at that date. In rather the same way a history written then praises what people admired at the time. We always tend to praise what we ourselves think would go well, and to put a piece like; so in looking at the jigsaw puzzle of the past it is always tempting to put a piece where we think it would go well, and to think that the whole picture is far simpler and tidier than, so far as we can tell, it was.

Below: Maiden Castle, in Dorset in south-west England. This ridge overlooking the countryside around, was a good place to live. In the 2000s BC Stone-Age people built huts and a ditched enclosure for their animals there. At this time the country round was wooded marshes, and the ridge provided farmland. About 2000 BC a vast long barrow (burial mound) was built on the highest point. A little later Bronze-Age people settled there. By about 1500 BC the bogs and swamps below had dried out and the land could be farmed. The ridge was deserted until the 5th century BC when a fort was built there, surrounded by walls of earth and chalk and outside them a wide, deep ditch.

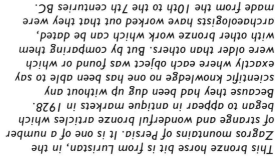

This bronze horse bit is from Luristan, in the Zagros mountains of Persia. It is one of a number of strange and wonderful bronze articles which began to appear in antique markets in 1928. Because they had been dug up without any scientific knowledge no one has been able to say exactly where each object was found or which were older than others. But by comparing them with other bronze work which can be dated, archaeologists have worked out that they were made from the 10th to the 7th centuries BC.

This relief shows the pharaoh Ramesses II holding Nubian prisoners by the hair. The inscription around the picture tells of his campaigns. But inscriptions like these can be unreliable, and historians have learned not to trust them. Often they paint a falsely glorious picture of a ruler's deeds.

The First Men

Who were the first 'men'? No one can answer this question exactly. Scholars have traced our ancestors right back to small, furry, tree-living creatures who were also ancestors of apes and monkeys. But at some time Man's ancestors split off from the others. They became able to walk upright and their brains became larger. They began to make and use tools and they learned to speak.

All we know about the earliest men is what we can learn from their bones and from the objects they made. So far only a few early sites have been studied. But more and more skeletons are being found which help to build up a picture of our ancestors' gradual development from creatures little different from apes to people who, though primitive cave-dwelling hunters, were physically just like us.

The first real men lived in Africa about 2 million years ago. Living in the same areas were creatures called 'near-men'. Although the near-men walked upright, they were vegetarians, with smaller brains and bigger back teeth than the first true men. The near-men probably came from the same ancestors as men, but evolved in a different way. They probably died out over a million years ago. In this scene a group of early men are working near a lake. Cautiously looking at them from behind some rocks is a group of near-men. Such groups probably kept away from each other as they lived in very different ways.

1 The first men to reach America probably got there overland! During the Ice Ages there was a wide land bridge between Asia and Alaska. Some people think they arrived there 30,000 years ago, probably following herds of migrating animals. They had reached the tip of South America 11,000 years ago.

2 People living at Terra Amata in southern France about 300,000 years ago built camps with huts made from wooden poles and stones, roofed with hide or branches. They used stone 'hand axes' and were skilled hunters, killing elephants, wild boars, and rhinoceroses.

Flint spearhead

Hand axe

3 From about 100,000 to 30,000 years ago, people known as Neanderthal Men were living in Europe and the Near East. They are named after the valley in Germany where their remains were first found. They had large noses and no chins, and their brains were sometimes even larger than those of modern men! In certain ways they were so like us that some people think they were our ancestors. Other people think they died out, leaving no descendants.

Painted pebble, France and Spain

Hand axe

Between about 16,000 and 10,000 BC southern Europe was inhabited by hunting peoples. Deep in caves in France and northern Spain they painted brilliantly coloured and detailed pictures of the animals they hunted. This painting, from Altamira in Spain, shows a bison. It was probably done about 15,000 years ago.

Siberian bone necklace

5 About 500,000 years ago people known as Peking Men were living in north China. Similar people were living in Java. They ate animals (such as deer and rhinoceros), fruits, and seeds. Probably they used fire to cook their meat.

Peking Man

Pebble-tool from Olduvai

6 About 30,000 years ago our ancestors were living at Cro-Magnon in southern France. These were the first people just like us. They lived in rock shelters, often with inner tents of skins. They had skin clothes, roughly sewn together. They carved ornaments out of stone and bone, and deep inside caves they painted wonderful pictures of the animals they hunted.

4 The first 'men' appeared in eastern Africa about 2 million years ago. They made crude stone tools and probably ate meat. They may have built stone structures – perhaps as windbreaks or as part of simple huts.

7 About 30,000 years ago men were living near Lake Mungo in south-east Australia. They must have travelled about 80 kilometres (50 miles) across water to get to Australia.

This blade, shaped like a laurel-leaf, was skilfully flaked from flint. It was made about 19,000 to 15,000 years ago, by people living in France. Stone-Age hunters made really efficient tools by striking flakes from rocks.

The First Religions

From very early times people have had to come to terms with happenings which they could not explain but which deeply affected their lives – events like the seasons, disease, birth, and death, and the migrations of animals they hunted. In all parts of the world, religions have grown up based on efforts to understand the unknown.

Early Gods
Neanderthal men, who lived between 100,000 and about 30,000 years ago, carefully buried their dead. Sometimes they put flowers, or animal bones and flint tools, with them. The Cro-Magnon people who followed them in Europe made skilfully carved and modelled figures of animals and women. Deep inside their caves they painted pictures of the animals they hunted. People think that these very early communities already had special ceremonies to do with death, and to bring them success in hunting.

Perhaps during that time people were already thinking that all sorts of things, such as the Sun and Moon and special places and objects, had their own spirits, or gods and goddesses. These spirits could be influenced if they were approached in the right way, and with the right sort of ceremony. This is certainly the way in which many simple peoples, who lived in places cut off from developing civilizations, have thought until the present day.

Unfortunately, we can know very little for sure. Early religious practices were not written down, but handed on from generation to generation by example. In areas where people settled down to a way of life which depended on farming, customs and ceremonies must have gradually changed. Ceremonies designed to make sure of good hunting, for instance, would slowly have given way to others meant to produce a good harvest.

Organized Religion
The earliest religion of which we have definite knowledge is that of the city-states of Sumer. Here religious ceremonies became especially important and closely linked to the ways in which the states were governed.

In Sumer there was an ancient tradition of building temples to local nature gods who protected the crops from flood and drought. Some of these temples became the centres around which the first cities grew up. The god of the temple grew in importance to become the protector of the city. The ruler of a Sumerian city kept the city god friendly by building more temples, and by performing the ceremonies the god required. In return the god protected the city in peace and war.

The cat was considered a sacred animal by the ancient Egyptians. In this papyrus from Thebes, made about 1300 BC, a cat cuts up the serpent Apophis who had attacked the sun-god Ra.

This female figure, dating from about 5750 BC, was found at Çatal Hüyük in Anatolia. Figures like these are found at ancient sites far away from one another. They suggest that some sort of mother-goddess was worshipped by early people.

This seal is from the Indus Valley civilization of northern India (about 2500–1750 BC). It shows Pashupali, lord of the animals, seated in a cross-legged position. This posture and the three faces of the god remain elements in the Hindu tradition of a thousand years later.

In Egypt, too, early farmers worshipped local nature gods. Later, after Upper and Lower Egypt were joined together, these gods became associated with the power and glories of the Egyptian kings. One local nature god, Amun of Thebes, rose in importance to become the king of the gods – this was because a family of kings from Thebes came into power.

Myths and Legends
All over the world, early peoples made up stories to explain how the world and the things in it began. These stories are usually called 'myths', from a Greek word meaning 'a story of the gods'.

The Near East produced many myths. This was the region where the change from village farming to highly organized states first took place. Old religious traditions were altered to fit a world in which warfare between states, and violent invasions by peoples outside the civilized areas, were common events.

This complicated world also showed in stories of gods and goddesses, who quarrelled among themselves for power just like human rulers. Over 2000 years such myths built up and overlapped: often different countries had very similar myths about their own gods.

Greek and Roman Mythology
The Greeks borrowed stories from Near Eastern and Egyptian myths and peopled them with the Greek family of gods and goddesses. In the 7th century BC a Greek writer called Hesiod wrote a long poem in which he explained how all the gods came to be born and what each god did.

The Greeks thought that their gods, like the thunder-god Zeus, the sea-god Poseidon, and the moon-goddess Artemis, must have shown themselves to different peoples in different forms. So to the Greeks the Egyptian god Amun was a form of Zeus, and the Great Goddess of the Ephesians was a form of Artemis.

The Romans were deeply attracted by the beautiful stories of the Greek gods, and they adapted their own gods to the Greek system. So the Roman Jupiter became identified with Greek Zeus, Roman Neptune with Greek Poseidon, and so on.

Eastern Ways of Life

In India and China, conditions were right for the growth of great systems of thought (*philosophies*) in which every kind of belief and practice had a place. One reason for this was the sheer size of the areas involved. With so many people having different beliefs it was impossible to impose a single set of beliefs upon them. Instead, such systems accepted that people must continue to worship in their own ways.

Hinduism, the first great religion of India, dates back to well before 1000 BC. It teaches of a single world spirit, Brahman, of which all gods, people, and things are part. All sorts of gods and beliefs come within its framework. Its law of *Dharma* teaches that people must obey the divine order of the universe. Each person is born into a certain position in life, and must work to fulfil the tasks laid down for him. If he does so, he will be rewarded by being born again into a higher position.

In the 6th century BC, three great philosophies developed in the East. They were Buddhism, Confucianism, and Taoism, and they taught that people must accept things as they are and work hard to live correctly.

Buddhism was developed by a great Indian teacher, Gautama, who lived from about 563 to 483 BC. Gautama was known as the Buddha (the Enlightened One), and he taught that men could only escape the pain and suffering of life on Earth by obeying certain great rules. One of the rules was that people should not harm any living thing. This rule was called *Ahimsa*.

A row of sculptured lions on the island of Delos. They guard the lake where the god Apollo was said to have been born. This island was one of the most sacred places of ancient Greece, and had temples to Apollo and several other gods.

China, too, had great spiritual teachers. The two greatest were Confucius, born about 551 BC, and Lao-Tze, who lived about the same time. Confucius said that order, good conduct towards people of higher rank, and setting a good example were very important. In this way, he thought, society would be made perfect.

Lao-Tze wrote down the basic ideas of Taoism. The word Tao means 'the Way', or the principle on which nature works. By following the Way, people can live in peace and harmony with the world.

All these philosophies, in one form or another, have survived into the modern world. All of them were rooted in the unchanging nature of life in the East where the most important fact was the unceasing round of planting and harvesting the crops.

One God

Of all the religions of the ancient world only one – Judaism – developed the idea of a single, all-powerful god. This being revealed himself to Abraham, the ancestor of the Jewish people. God entered into an agreement with his chosen people. If they would obey certain laws, he would protect them.

Judaism was the ancestor of Christianity. Christians accept the great Jewish religious writings called the Old Testament. But they believe, as Jews do not, that Jesus Christ was the promised Son of God, born into the world to save mankind. Christianity soon spread through the Roman world.

Another great religion with close links to Judaism is Islam, or Submission to the Will of God, or Allah. Muslims (as the followers of Islam are known) respect the Jewish scriptures and the teachings of Jesus, whom they regard as a prophet. Islam was founded in Arabia by Muhammad, in the 7th century AD. It spread rapidly to divide the old Mediterranean world into Christian Europe, and Islamic Africa and Asia.

The Chinese philosopher Confucius, who lived in the 6th century BC. He taught that, in dealing with other people: 'What you do not want done to yourself, do not do to others.'

A Peruvian gold figure of a puma, dating from the 4th to 9th centuries AD. On its back is a design of sacred two-headed snakes. The 'Cult of the Cat', shown in snarling fanged masks of pumas and jaguars, began in Peru in the last few centuries BC.

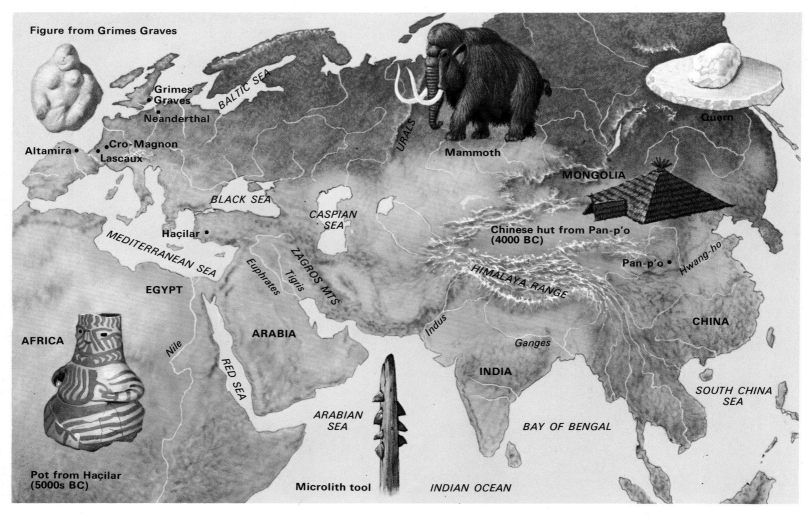

Figure from Grimes Graves

Grimes Graves

Neanderthal

Altamira

Cro-Magnon
Lascaux

BALTIC SEA

Mammoth

Quern

URALS

MONGOLIA

BLACK SEA

CASPIAN SEA

Chinese hut from Pan-p'o (4000 BC)

Haçilar

MEDITERRANEAN SEA

Euphrates

ZAGROS MTS

Tigris

HIMALAYA RANGE

Pan-p'o

Hwang-ho

EGYPT

AFRICA

Nile

RED SEA

ARABIA

Indus

Ganges

CHINA

INDIA

SOUTH CHINA SEA

ARABIAN SEA

BAY OF BENGAL

Pot from Haçilar (5000s BC)

Microlith tool

INDIAN OCEAN

From Hunters to Farmers

More than 35,000 years ago the world was deep in the grip of the last great Ice Age. In the northern hemisphere, vast ice sheets stretched from the North Pole to cover much of what is now Britain and northern Europe. The huge area of ice meant that the climate of the world was very different from that of today. Central Europe, for example, was a type of semi-frozen treeless desert, called tundra, which today is only found within the Arctic Circle. Even the shape of the land was different. So much water was locked up in the ice that the sea level was much lower. Areas of land now separated by the sea were joined together by land bridges.

Man in the Ice Age

The people who lived in the Ice Age were hunters. They used tools and weapons made of flint, skilfully chipped into shape. With these they hunted down and killed the big game animals which wandered in great herds over the Earth. In the cold lands of the north, herds of woolly mammoth, caribou, mastodon, and moose provided meat for food and skins for clothing and shelter. Further south were herds of elephant, tapir, wild pig, and deer.

The hunters of these times had no settled homes, so that we have very little knowledge of them. What we do know is based on scattered finds of tools and food remains left behind at temporary encampments. A camp might be occupied for a few days or a few months, and when the wild herds moved on in search of new feeding grounds, the hunters followed.

One site at Cro-Magnon in France has given its name to a group of hunters who spread westwards from the Near East about 30,000 BC. The Cro-Magnons may have been the first modern men – our direct ancestors. As they moved westwards across Europe they may have met a different type of man. This type, called Neanderthal Man after the site in Germany where the first remains were found, may have gradually died out.

Paintings of animals from a cave at Lascaux, in southern France. They date from 16,000 to 10,000 BC: in those times people lived by hunting.

Left: Even today there are still people who depend on migrating animals for food, clothing, and shelter. These Lapps follow herds of reindeer as they move through northern Scandinavia.

The Cro-Magnon people were skilled hunters and toolmakers. They fashioned fine tools and weapons out of flint, stone, bone, ivory, and the antlers of deer. The animals they hunted gave them meat for food and skins for clothes and tents. These, of course, have not survived, but we *can* get an idea of how advanced the Cro-Magnon people were. Deep in special caves at sites like Lascaux and Altamira (see page 11) they painted extraordinary pictures of the animals they hunted.

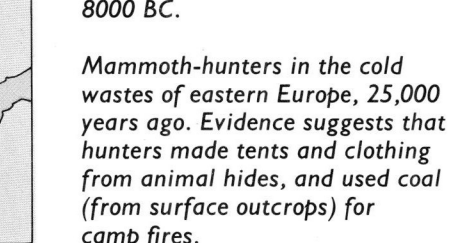

A woman's head, delicately carved from mammoth ivory as early as 22,000 BC. She may be wearing a type of headdress, or perhaps some special hairstyle. It was found in France.

Left: The Fertile Crescent – the region in the Near East where farming first developed, about 8000 BC.

Mammoth-hunters in the cold wastes of eastern Europe, 25,000 years ago. Evidence suggests that hunters made tents and clothing from animal hides, and used coal (from surface outcrops) for camp fires.

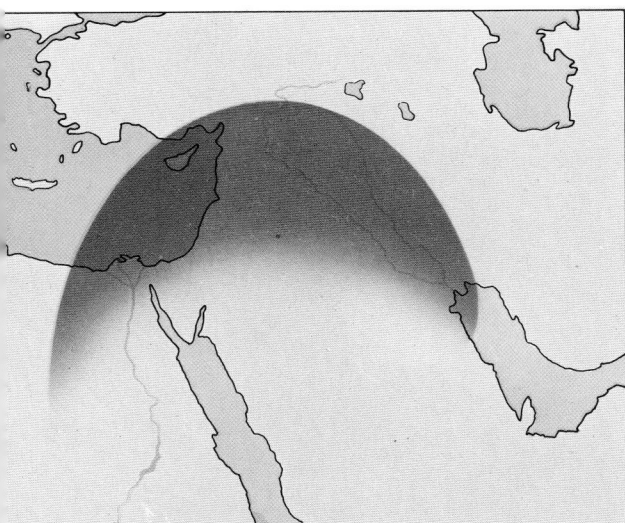

The End of the Ice Age

Towards 10,000 BC the Ice Age came to an end. The great ice sheets slowly melted and shrank northwards, bringing enormous changes to the world. Europe, which had been an arctic desert, became covered with thick forest and woodland. North Africa became an area with heavy rainfall, before drying up into the great deserts of today. The melting ice caused enormous amounts of water to flow into the oceans and the sea level rose. Many parts of the world were cut off by the rising oceans, leaving people and animals in those areas to develop in very different ways.

In Europe and Asia, many of the big mammals which had survived the Ice Age were slowly hunted to extinction. Others, like bison, elk, and reindeer, moved farther north to stay with the tundra. By 10,000 BC, hunters had to depend on smaller game – fish, deer, wild pig, and wildfowl. They developed a great variety of weapons and tools, such as the bow and arrow, for hunting different kinds of animals. They also added to their food supply by gathering wild fruits and berries in the forests. Some peoples made permanent homes by shallow coastal waters where there was a plentiful supply of shellfish.

THE FIRST FARMERS

In many parts of the world people carried on a hunting and gathering life for thousands of years. But about 8000 BC, important developments took place in the Near East. Here men learned first to harvest the wild grains that grew in the area, and then to sow them. The early farmers made flint sickles to cut the wild grain, and primitive millstones (called querns) to separate the grain from the husks. For the first time, men began to rely on food that they grew themselves, and to domesticate wild sheep, goats, pigs, and cattle.

The World in 3000 BC

By now, settled farming has developed in many parts of the world. Villages have grown up whose people often make beautifully painted pottery. Metalworking – first of natural copper and gold, and then of copper smelted from ores and bronze – is spreading out from Anatolia (Asia Minor) where it developed. The two most advanced areas are Mesopotamia and Egypt; in both regions cities and temples are being built, writing systems have been developed, and skills including sculpture and metalworking are increasing rapidly.

This frog was carved in Egypt in the 3000s BC.

1 The Americas Most of the people are still living by hunting and food gathering, but in Central America and Peru beans and maize are beginning to be cultivated. On the coast of Ecuador is a town of 3000 people – farmers, fishers, and craftsmen.

2 Egypt Upper (south) and Lower (north) Egypt are joined about 3100 under Menes (Narmer). Main gods are established and worshipped in elaborate temples and shrines. Gold- and copper-working increase rapidly; hieroglyphic writing is developed.

A village on the river Nile in the 3000s BC. The papyrus reeds growing on the river banks were used for making huts and even for boats.

Peruvian hut

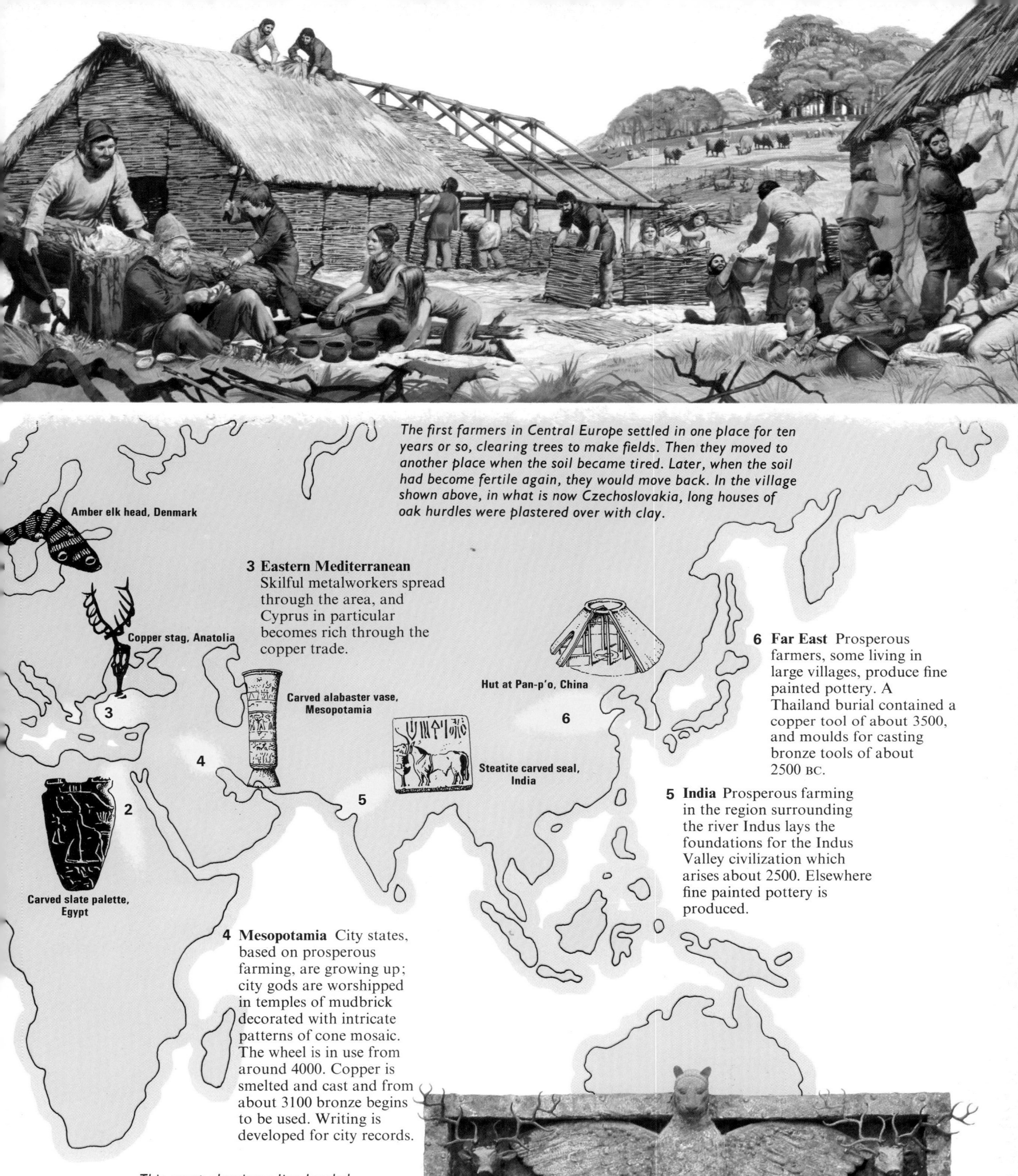

The first farmers in Central Europe settled in one place for ten years or so, clearing trees to make fields. Then they moved to another place when the soil became tired. Later, when the soil had become fertile again, they would move back. In the village shown above, in what is now Czechoslovakia, long houses of oak hurdles were plastered over with clay.

Amber elk head, Denmark

Copper stag, Anatolia

3 Eastern Mediterranean Skilful metalworkers spread through the area, and Cyprus in particular becomes rich through the copper trade.

Carved alabaster vase, Mesopotamia

Hut at Pan-p'o, China

Steatite carved seal, India

Carved slate palette, Egypt

6 Far East Prosperous farmers, some living in large villages, produce fine painted pottery. A Thailand burial contained a copper tool of about 3500, and moulds for casting bronze tools of about 2500 BC.

5 India Prosperous farming in the region surrounding the river Indus lays the foundations for the Indus Valley civilization which arises about 2500. Elsewhere fine painted pottery is produced.

4 Mesopotamia City states, based on prosperous farming, are growing up; city gods are worshipped in temples of mudbrick decorated with intricate patterns of cone mosaic. The wheel is in use from around 4000. Copper is smelted and cast and from about 3100 bronze begins to be used. Writing is developed for city records.

This group showing a lion-headed eagle and two stags is made of hammered copper sheet. It comes from a Sumerian temple in Iraq, and dates from the 3000s BC. It is 2·4 metres (8 feet) long and just over 1 metre (39 inches) high.

Mastering Skills

When we look at ancient history, we usually look at each area of the world in turn. We see how its civilization grew up, how it became powerful, and how it eventually fell. This is an easy way to learn about things. But another way of looking at the past is to study developments that were common to many different civilizations. Examples of such things are metalworking, pottery, the use of money, and writing systems.

These developments did not happen overnight. They were the results of perhaps thousands of years of experience. Sometimes, as in the case of metalworking, the same discoveries were made separately in quite different parts of the world. Sometimes a similar need led to very different developments, such as the variety of writing systems worked out by different civilizations.

Metalworking

Wherever metalworking developed, it became important to people in controlling their surroundings. Once metal tools were invented, it was easier and quicker to clear and cultivate land, and to work a wider range of materials. Metal weapons, produced in large quantities, allowed rulers to equip great armies.

The earliest metals to be worked were copper, silver, and gold in the Near East – especially in Anatolia (Asia Minor), which had rich sources of these metals. As early as the 7000s BC, nuggets of metal found on the ground surface were hammered into small pins, fishhooks, and trinkets.

True metalworking in the Near East did not begin until about 4500 BC. Only then did people learn how to heat copper-bearing rock to a temperature high enough to melt out the pure metal. Molten copper was then

poured into moulds to make tools like axe-heads, spearheads, chisels, and so on. But copper is a rather soft metal; it needs frequent hammering and reheating if it is to keep a sharp edge. Copper tools were not as good as tools and weapons made of flint and obsidian (volcanic glass) which were already in existence.

Not until about 3000 BC did the Near Eastern metalworkers learn how to make copper much harder, by adding a small amount of a much rarer and more expensive metal – tin. The mixture that resulted is called bronze.

Copper- and bronze-working spread only slowly from centres in the Near East. It cost a lot to make tools from the metals and only the highly organized and wealthy societies of the region could afford to employ skilled craftsmen. In undeveloped northern Europe, for example, bronze-working did not begin until about 1000 BC.

In other parts of the world, metalworking began later than in the Near East. It spread to the Indus Valley after 2500 BC. In China, bronze-working had developed independently by 1500 BC. But in the Americas true metalworking was unknown until the 4th century BC.

Iron

In the Near East, it was more than 1500 years from the start of the Bronze Age to the start of iron production. This was because iron was very difficult to work. One problem was that iron-bearing rocks had to be heated to very high temperatures in order to separate the metal from the rock. The result was still not molten iron, but a spongy mass which had to be heated and hammered for a long time.

In the eastern Mediterranean area skilled craftsmen were working iron in about 1200 BC; iron implements are found in Europe dating from about 1000 BC. Iron-working developed independently in the Ganges Valley of India (about 1000 BC) and in China (about 600 BC). The Chinese developed cast iron (melting the ore and pouring it into moulds) about 1800 years before the Europeans.

Money

It is hard for us today to think of buying anything without paying for it in coins of a fixed value. Yet coinage did not develop until about 700 BC in the Near East, long after the beginning of civilization. Until then people paid for goods in a variety of ways. Some used tokens, such as shells or beads. Others used ingots of metals like copper, bronze, and iron, or even paid with livestock, such as cattle and horses. This still happens in parts of the world today.

This wallpainting from an Egyptian tomb shows metalworkers. They are using bellows worked by foot to get a hot enough fire to melt the copper and tin for bronze. It dates from about 1500 BC.

This pot, shaped like an animal, was made in China around 2000 BC. It is much like a pot made in South America in about 500 AD by the Mochica people (see page 56).

An early coin from Phrygia in Anatolia (Asia Minor). It is made of electrum, an alloy (mixture) of gold and silver.

This huge storage jar, or pithos, was found at Knossos in Crete. Jars like this were used for storing grain, oil, and wine. For thousands of years jars of many sizes were used as containers, and many of them were sent abroad when they contained exports.

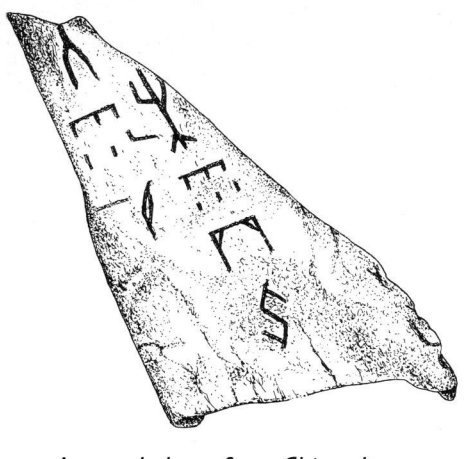

An oracle bone from China. It dates from the Shang period, about 1500 BC. Oracle bones were used for telling the future. The drawings on them are a very early form of modern Chinese writing. The Shang script had characters like small pictures, but over the centuries these have changed so that now Chinese characters are not usually at all like the objects or ideas they represent.

The Sumerian cuneiform script was adapted to write many Near Eastern languages. The writing on this seal is in the Elamite language. It comes from the 6th or 5th century BC.

A tablet from Knossos showing writing in the Linear B script, used by the Mycenaeans. Until 1952 no one could read this script. Then a British architect called Michael Ventris worked out that it was used for writing a very early form of Greek.

Right: An Egyptian papyrus of the 13th century BC. The written language of the Egyptians is called hieroglyphic. It was made up of picture symbols which sometimes represented objects or ideas, and sometimes represented consonants. A simplified form of hieroglyphic called 'hieratic' was developed in about 1900 BC. In about 700 BC a popular ('demotic') script was developed which was much faster to write.

The first known use of money was in the kingdom of Lydia, in Anatolia, in the 7th century BC. The Lydian 'coins' were thick oval pieces of precious metal, stamped with a symbol showing their fixed weight.

From Lydia their use spread to the Greek cities of the Anatolian coasts, and from there to mainland Greece itself. These early coins were too valuable for everyday use – just one might have paid for a whole boat-load of goods. But by the 5th century BC it was becoming usual to issue coins of smaller value for day-to-day use, and payment in money was becoming common.

Pottery

Even 25,000 years ago, hunters made small clay models of the animals they hunted. But wandering hunters and food gatherers could not carry heavy, breakable clay pots with them. The first pottery vessels were not made until the 7000s BC, when village life developed in the Near East. Everywhere in the world, pottery is linked to the growth of settled, village communities.

Early pots were made by pressing a slab of sandy clay over a rounded object, or by coiling a long roll of clay on top of a flat base. The sides were then smoothed, and the finished pots dried in the sun before being baked hard in a fire. Later, special ovens called kilns were made, in which pots could be fired at controlled temperatures.

In the 4000s BC came another important development – the potter's wheel. Rotating the clay on a simple turntable made it easier to shape. The potter's wheel was in use in the Aegean area by 2000 BC – but it only reached Europe after 1000 BC.

Writing

Even though there are thousands of different spoken languages in the world, only a very few writing systems have developed.

The first known writing system came about in Sumer in about 3000 BC. It developed to meet the need to make records of the complicated transactions of huge land-owning organizations like temples and palaces. In the beginning Sumerian 'writing' was no more than a number of simplified

picture symbols of the objects that they stood for. They were pressed into tablets of soft river clay with reed 'pens'. The clay was then dried in the sun.

As time went on, however, the Sumerian picture-writing developed until it could record not only simple lists of objects, but the language that people actually spoke. An important change came about when a picture symbol could stand not only for an object, but the *sound* of the word for that object. The first picture symbols gave way to a kind of shorthand version of them, which was quicker and easier to write. It was made up of triangular marks in the clay tablets. It is called *cuneiform* (wedge-shaped) script, from the Latin word *cuneus*, a wedge.

In Egypt, a rather different form of picture writing developed about 3000 BC. Not long afterwards the Egyptians invented a kind of paper made from the split and flattened stems of the papyrus reed. This meant that from early on the Egyptians painted their *hieroglyphic* script on to a smooth surface, and it became flowing and decorative.

The Alphabet

Between 1600 and 1000 BC a new writing system grew up in the Near East. This was the alphabetic system. Although there were various forms, all had the advantage that they needed fewer signs to write a language.

Scripts like Egyptian hieroglyphic and cuneiform were *syllabic*: each sign stood for the sound of a whole word, or part of a word. The alphabet, on the other hand, used a single sign for each sound in a word. Egyptian and cuneiform systems had many hundreds of signs, but an alphabetic system needed fewer than 30.

By the 10th century BC a fully alphabetic system was in use in the Phoenician city of Tyre. It may have been from the Phoenicians that the ancient Greeks adopted the alphabet in the 8th or early 7th century BC. Our word 'alphabet' itself is made up of the first two signs of the Greek alphabet, alpha (α) and beta (β). Because the Greeks used the alphabet, all modern European languages are written with the alphabetic system.

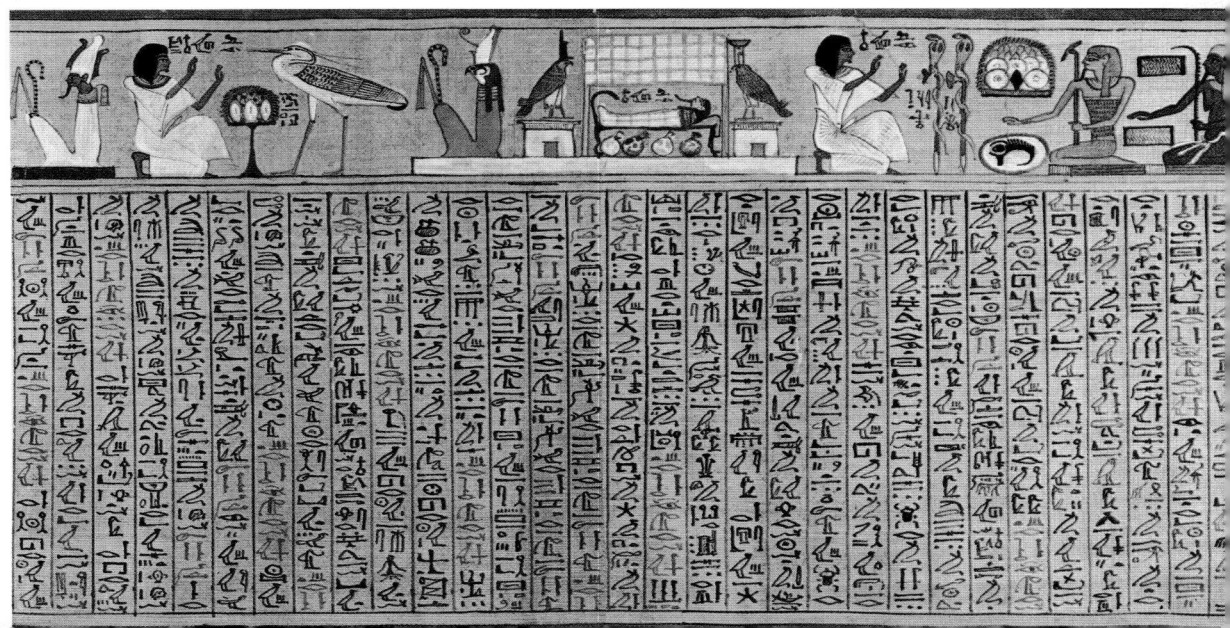

ANATOLIA

TAURUS MTS

SYRIAN DESERT

PALESTINE

ASSYRIA
• Nineveh
• Kalah
• Ashur

Euphrates

Tigris

Mari •

Agade ?

AMURRU

Babylon •

AKKADIA

SUMER
• Lagash
Uruk •
• Ur
Eridu •

PERSIA

ZAGROS MTS

ELAM

ARABIAN GULF

Assyrian hunters
(7th century BC)

Ruler of Lagash
(2150 BC)

Mesopotamia

BC	CHRONOLOGY
c3100	Great temples built in Sumer. Earliest writing at Uruk
c2700–2400	Sumerian cities fortified and ruled by kings. Constant warfare
2371–2255	Akkadian empire, founded by Sargon
2113–2006	Third Dynasty of Ur rules Sumer

Mesopotamia is a Greek word which means 'the land between the rivers'. It is used to describe the region between the rivers Tigris and Euphrates, the southern area of which is mainly low-lying swamp and marshland. It was here, in what is now the southern part of the state of Iraq, that one of the world's first civilizations grew up between 4000 and 3000 BC.

The fertile lands of Mesopotamia lie between the desert and the mountains. To the west are the vast Arabian and Syrian deserts: to the east the Zagros mountains rise to 3000 metres (10,000 feet). Mesopotamia itself falls into two main regions. The northern part has a regular rainfall. The south, stretching down to the Arabian Gulf, suffers dry, scorching summers from May to October. This area, once called Sumer, is a flat plain built up from layers of mud carried there by the rivers when they flooded. The soil is fertile, but needs to be watered (irrigated) if it is to grow crops. Because the area is so flat, it is often threatened by violent floods.

The marshlands of ancient Sumer (now southern Iraq) saw the growth of the world's first cities. Today communities of Marsh Arabs (right) live lives that may not be very different from those of the early Sumerians. The Marsh Arabs use reeds to build houses and boats and even as food: fish and dates are important sources of food today, just as they were 6000 years ago. Some people think that the Marsh Arabs may be the descendants of the ancient Sumerians.

From Villages to Cities

Farming spread slowly all over western Asia. By 5000 BC there were many large, prosperous villages – almost towns. Between 4000 and 3500 BC, however, the farming peoples of Sumer made the greatest step forward of all. From living in villages they developed to build the world's first true cities at sites like Ur and Eridu.

Sumer is a flat, swampy area of southern Mesopotamia about the size of the Netherlands. Although the soil is fertile river mud, the ancient Sumerian farmers faced many difficulties. There was no rainfall, so they had to dig irrigation canals to water their fields. For seven months the sun was burning hot: it drew the moisture from the ground, leaving it salty and infertile. In the spring, just as the crops were ripe, the rivers often flooded disastrously, swamping the fields and threatening the harvest.

But Sumer had important natural resources. Date palms grew well even in salty ground. In the marshes were wild pig and wildfowl, and there were fish from the rivers. These extra sources of food could support a large population. The more people there were, the better they could dig and clean the canals, and build dams to control the floods.

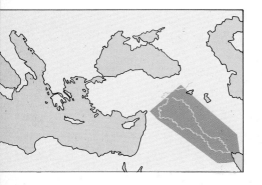

Trade and Empire

Between 2800 and 2400 BC, the city-states of Sumer were at their strongest and most wealthy. At different times, one city or another became powerful enough to rule the others. Sumer became the richest market in the world, attracting trade from the eastern Mediterranean to the Indus Valley.

But the wealth of Sumer also attracted greedy eyes. Just to the north, in the area of Agade, the ruler Sargon had become very powerful through his control of the trade routes to the north, west, and east. In about 2350 BC, Sargon attacked Sumer and made it part of his huge empire. His capital, Agade, gives us the name by which Sargon's empire is known – the Akkadian empire. The Akkadian empire was the first attempt to unite a huge area under the rule of one man. From now on Mesopotamia was nearly always dominated by one, or at the most two, powerful states.

At the same time local centres, including temples, grew up. The temples were dedicated to the local god, who protected the people from floods and gave them a good harvest. The temples stored produce, either for food or for replanting at the start of the new growing season in October. They kept herds of animals, like the oxen and donkeys needed to draw ploughs. It is possible that the temples hired out these animals to farmers in return for a part of the crop.

The temples grew rich, and some cities were ruled by a temple official with the help of a staff of officials and scribes. Writing and counting systems were developed in order to keep track of the goods passing into and out of the storehouses. Two of the ruler's tasks were to build new temples to the god, and to maintain the irrigation system. These temples became the starting point for growing cities. Not only temple officials lived there but also the craftsmen who built and maintained the temples, merchants, and scribes. Sumer became a patchwork of independent cities, each supplied with food by its surrounding area of countryside.

The Sumerian city-states were often at war. This inscribed stone was put up to celebrate a great victory by the city of Lagash, under its ruler Eannatum (about 2500 BC), over its rival city of Umma. Two scenes are shown: at the top, Eannatum, in a garment of animal skins, leads a close formation of troops. Below: Eannatum, in his four-wheeled chariot, aims his lance at the enemy.

Right: A bronze head of an Akkadian king. The Akkadian empire grew to include all of Mesopotamia, and parts of North Syria and Elam (in south-west Iran). It was the first recorded attempt to administer such a large area.

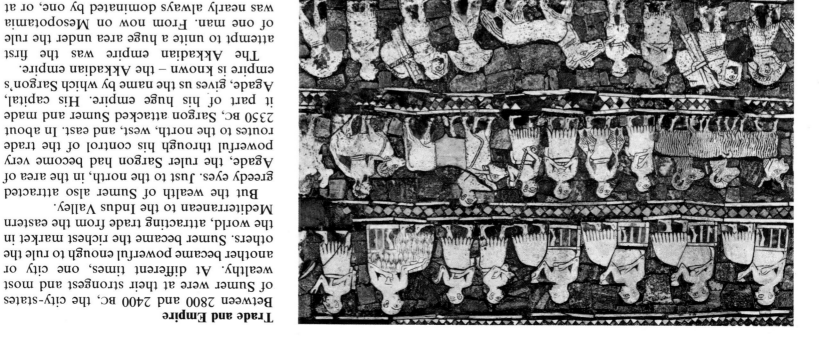

Part of the so-called 'Standard of Ur', perhaps the base of a harp. From about 2500 BC. The scenes show a society already divided into classes. At the top the rich sit at a feast. In the middle, servants drive cattle, sheep, and goats. At the bottom, labourers carry heavy loads. The figures are of shell and red limestone, set into a background of lapis lazuli with bitumen. Lapis lazuli, a semi-precious blue stone, was traded over long distances from sources in Afghanistan.

NATURAL RESOURCES

The Sumerians had no metal, stone, or wood of their own. These materials, together with precious metals, gem-stones, and other luxuries, were imported by way of the Arabian Gulf or overland from the north. The main resources of Sumer were deposits of clay and the river mud itself. Clay was used to make decorative bricks and pottery. Sumerian scribes wrote with reed 'pens' on soft clay writing tablets. The river mud was shaped into bricks and allowed to dry naturally in the scorching sun. Mudbrick was the main building material. Reeds were plentiful in the marshlands, and they were also useful: tied into bundles, they could be made into houses, boats, and rafts, as well as being woven into baskets and reed-mats. Bitumen, a kind of tar, was also important: it was used to fill cracks and make them watertight, and as a glue for inlay work.

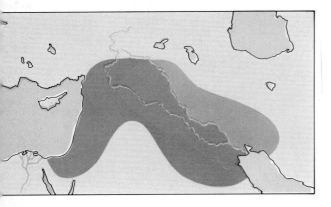

The map above shows the two Babylonian empires. The brown area is that ruled over by Hammurabi (1792–1750 BC) and later by the Kassites. The orange area is the Neo-(New) Babylonian empire, created by Nabopolassar (626–605 BC) and his son Nebuchadrezzar (605–562 BC). Between the two Babylonian empires came the period when Mesopotamia was ruled by the Assyrians. The map below shows their empire at its greatest extent, during the 7th century BC.

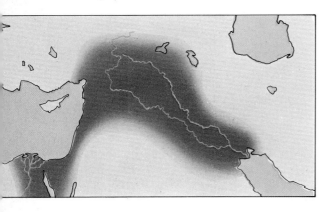

The First Empire
Sargon of Agade and his successors ruled the first empire that we know of. But size brought its own problems. Sargon's grandson, Naram-Sin, had to deal with many revolts by the peoples that he ruled. The Akkadian empire was also threatened by desert nomads in the west and hostile and warlike peoples of the Zagros mountains to the east.

The herders on the edge of the desert were not always hostile. But in times of severe drought they moved into the cultivated areas of the empire in search of grazing for their flocks. This naturally led to conflict.

In 2230 BC the Akkadian empire fell, because of these difficulties. For a while, part of south Mesopotamia was dominated by the Gutians, a mountain people the Sumerians called 'the Vipers from the Hills'. After a century of confusion Sumer, led by the kings of Ur's Third Dynasty, regained much of its former glory. But after only a hundred years, Ur was sacked by the strong state of Elam, to the east. At the same time, Sumer was invaded from the north by a Semitic people, the *amurru*, groups of whom settled in all the old Sumerian cities. Once again, Sumer suffered a period of weakness and confusion.

The Amorites
The *amurru*, or Amorites, were nomads living on the edge of the desert. Gradually some of them took over large areas of Mesopotamia, settling in cities like Mari, Ashur, and Babylon. When they became city-dwellers they absorbed the ways of Mesopotamia, and adapted the cuneiform script of the Sumerians and Akkadians (see page 19) to write their own language.

About 1760 BC, the great Hammurabi, the Amorite ruler of Babylon, attacked Mari and Ashur and became overlord of most of the city-states of northern and southern Mesopotamia. By the end of his reign in 1750 BC, he could describe himself as 'Mighty king, King of Babylon, King of the whole country of Amurru, King of Sumer and Akkad, King of the Four Quarters of the World'.

The Kassites
About 1600 BC Babylon was sacked by an Indo-European people, the Hittites, of central Anatolia to the north-west. In the confusion that followed, the Kassites – whose original home may have been in the Zagros mountains – seized the throne of Babylonia. Their power had much to do with their expert knowledge of horses: their two-wheeled horse-drawn chariots were the most advanced weapons of the time.

The Kassites ruled peacefully for 400 years. Under them, the cities of Babylonia came under central rule, but they were still thought of as important centres of religion, art, and literature. Babylonia developed into a national state, with Babylon as its administrative capital. But in 1150 Babylonia was devastated by a terrible raid by the Elamites. With great difficulty, new rulers in Babylon drove out the invaders, only to face a new threat from the warlike Assyrians to the north.

A black stone weight in the form of a duck. Setting up standard weights and measures was a way of carrying the power of a ruler into distant parts of his empire. This weight dates from the Third Dynasty of Ur.

A boundary stone, or 'kudurru', of the Kassite period in Babylonia (1590–1245 BC). Such stones were carved with prayers asking the gods to protect the owner's land.

A winged 'pazuzu' – a type of desert demon. The desert was the home of nomads who, from time to time, threatened the stability of the Mesopotamian states.

The Assyrians

The Assyrian homeland lay between the cities of Ashur and Nineveh on the river Tigris. From here, important trade routes led to Syria and Anatolia. For a long time the powerful rule of Babylonia to the south and the Hittites to the north-west prevented Assyria from expanding. But in the centuries following the collapse of the Hittite empire the Assyrians began to expand into the space left behind.

Under a strong king, Tiglathpileser III, in the 8th century, the Assyrian army was turned into a permanent, highly trained force. Over the next 50 years, the Assyrians conquered most of Syria, Palestine, and Phoenicia and invaded Egypt as far as Thebes (Luxor). Some regions became provinces; others were allowed to rule themselves under pro-Assyrian kings. The tribute and taxes that the Assyrians demanded led to terrible hardship. There were frequent revolts – which were savagely crushed. Land was left uncultivated, allowing hostile Aramaean herders to devastate whole areas of the empire.

An Assyrian king watches prisoners-of-war dragging a huge statue of a winged, human-headed bull from the stone quarries to his capital. Nearly every Assyrian king built himself a palace, or added greatly to an existing one. The wealth and labour needed to do so were drawn from the provinces of the Assyrian empire. This policy made the provinces poor and encouraged revolts. All the details in this reconstruction, including the sled, dragged along on rollers, and the raft, buoyed with inflated animal skins, are taken from Assyrian carvings.

THE NEO-BABYLONIAN EMPIRE

In Babylonia, a number of groups waged a desperate struggle to free themselves from Assyrian domination. Babylon itself was sacked by the Assyrian king, Sennacherib, and the population murdered. But the Babylonians fought on. Then about 631 civil war broke out in Assyria after the death of King Ashurbani-pal. Under Nabopolassar the Babylonians joined forces with the Medes of western Iran. Between 614 and 612 Assyria was invaded and the major cities Nineveh, Ashur, and Kalah were captured and destroyed. Nabopolassar's son Nebuchadrezzar II went on to conquer much of the old Assyrian empire. But after less than a century his Neo- (New) Babylonian empire surrendered to Persia.

1792–1750	Hammurabi king of Babylon
1590	Hittites raid Babylon
1590–1245	Kassites rule in Babylonia
1124–1103	Nebuchadrezzar I leads Babylonia's fight against Elam
745–c630	Assyrian empire at its height, ruled by strong kings like Sargon II, Sennacherib, Esarhaddon, Ashurbanipal
689	Babylon destroyed by Assyrians
626–605	Nabopolassar rules over Babylon and (after destroying Nineveh in 612) over the greater part of the former Assyrian empire
605–562	Nebuchadnezzar II king of Babylonia
597	Jerusalem falls to Babylonians
539	Nabonidus, last king of Babylonia, surrenders to Cyrus II of Persia

This reconstruction of the Ishtar Gate of Babylon uses the original glazed bricks. It dates from the Neo-Babylonian period, when Babylon was splendidly rebuilt.

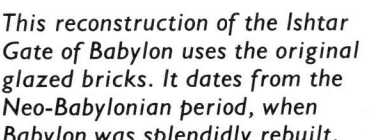

Egypt

The pyramids at Giza, seen across the green strip of the Cultivation. Farmland was so valuable in Egypt that great monuments like these were built in the desert, which begins where the fertile 'black earth' ends.

An Egyptian king was regarded as a god. This silver coffin of King Psusennes (about 1000 BC) shows him holding a crook and a flail, the symbols of his power to care for and punish his people.

BC	CHRONOLOGY
3100	Menes (?Narmer) unites Egypt
2686–2181	Old Kingdom
2650	Death of Zoser for whom first pyramid was built
2180–2040	First Intermediate Period. Absolute rule of kings disrupted by civil war
2040–1633	Middle Kingdom. Egyptian power extended southwards. Widespread trade with the Aegean and Levant
1633–1567	Second Intermediate Period. Egypt invaded by Hyksos peoples using horse-drawn chariots
1567–1085	New Kingdom. Hyksos driven from Egypt
1504–1450	Reign of Thutmosis III who wins a vast empire. Egyptian power at its greatest
1179	Ramesses III defeats foreign raiders known as 'Sea Peoples'
1087–751	Third Intermediate Period. Egypt ruled by Libyan, then Ethiopian invaders
751–332	Late Period. Times of independence alternate with conquest by Assyrians, then Persians, finally Alexander the Great (332). After his death Egypt is ruled by Alexander's general Ptolemy and his heirs
30	Egypt becomes a Roman province

Egypt is a hot, desert land, divided by the fertile valley of the river Nile. Hardly any rain falls there, and the summers are scorching hot. Even today, more than 90 per cent of Egypt is arid desert, where nothing can grow. But the strip of land, called the Cultivation, on each side of the Nile is one of the most fertile places in the world. Although it is no more than 20 kilometres ($12\frac{1}{2}$ miles) wide, it runs for about 1000 kilometres (620 miles) from Aswan in the south to the broad farmlands of the Delta, where the river runs into the Mediterranean.

The rich black soil of the Cultivation was laid down over thousands of years by the regular flooding of the Nile. The river used to burst its banks every year between June and October until modern dams were built to control it. The sticky black mud that the floodwaters left behind was so rich that two or even three crops could be grown in one season, as long as it was well-watered.

The Ancient Egyptians

Its fertile soil was the reason why, more than 5000 years ago, the Nile Valley saw the development of the brilliant civilization of the Ancient Egyptians. The earliest Egyptians had learned to farm the land along the banks, using water from the river to water their crops. The villages along the Nile grew rich and began to join together to help one another dig the ditches and dams needed to control the annual flooding.

In about 3100 BC a king called Menes united the whole of Egypt under his rule. He and his descendants were Egypt's first ruling family, or dynasty. The earliest period we know much about is called the Old Kingdom (2686–2181 BC). By this time the kings had become immensely powerful. Writing, painting, architecture, and crafts were highly developed. Egyptian power and influence flourished for almost 2000 years, despite two periods of civil war and foreign invasion.

At its greatest, under strong rulers like Thutmosis III (1504–1450 BC), Egypt controlled Palestine and Syria and reached southwards to the African state of Nubia. But by 1150 BC Egypt was surrounded by powerful enemies. In 935 a Libyan invader, Sheshonk I, seized the throne. Except for a period between 664 and 525 BC, Egypt was ruled by foreign kings until it was finally conquered by Rome in 30 BC.

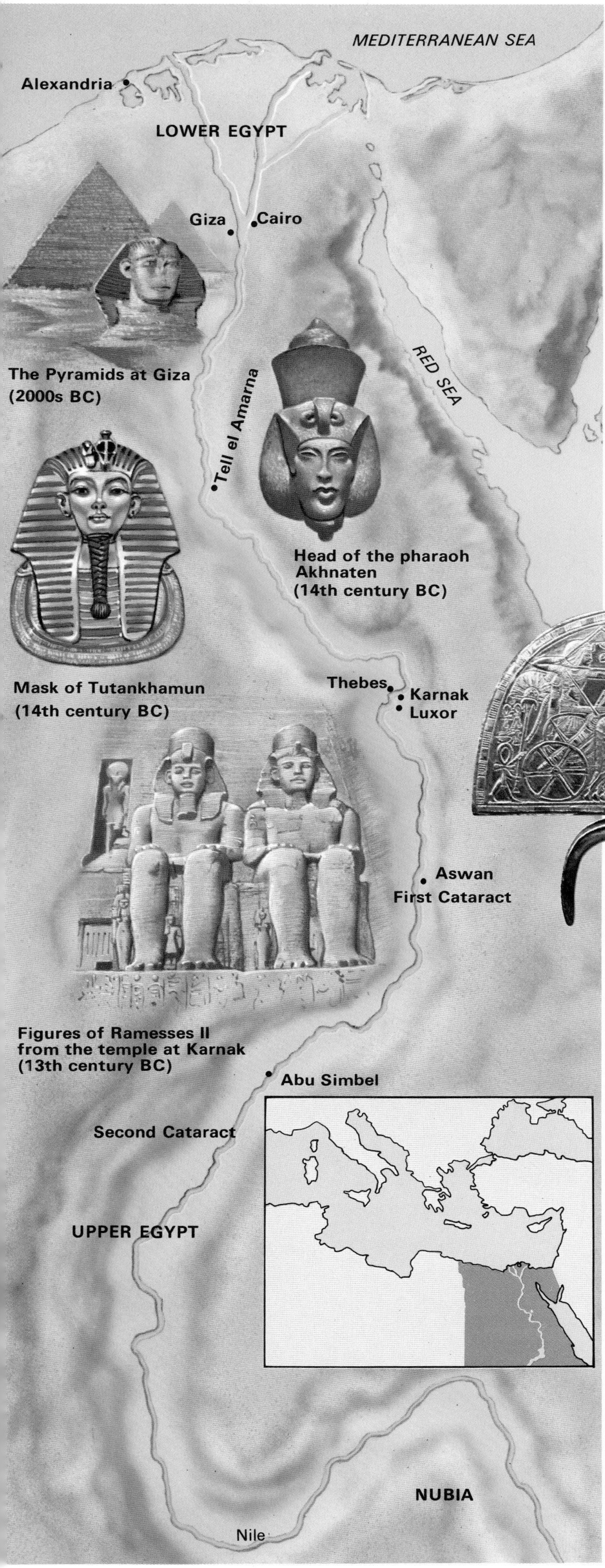

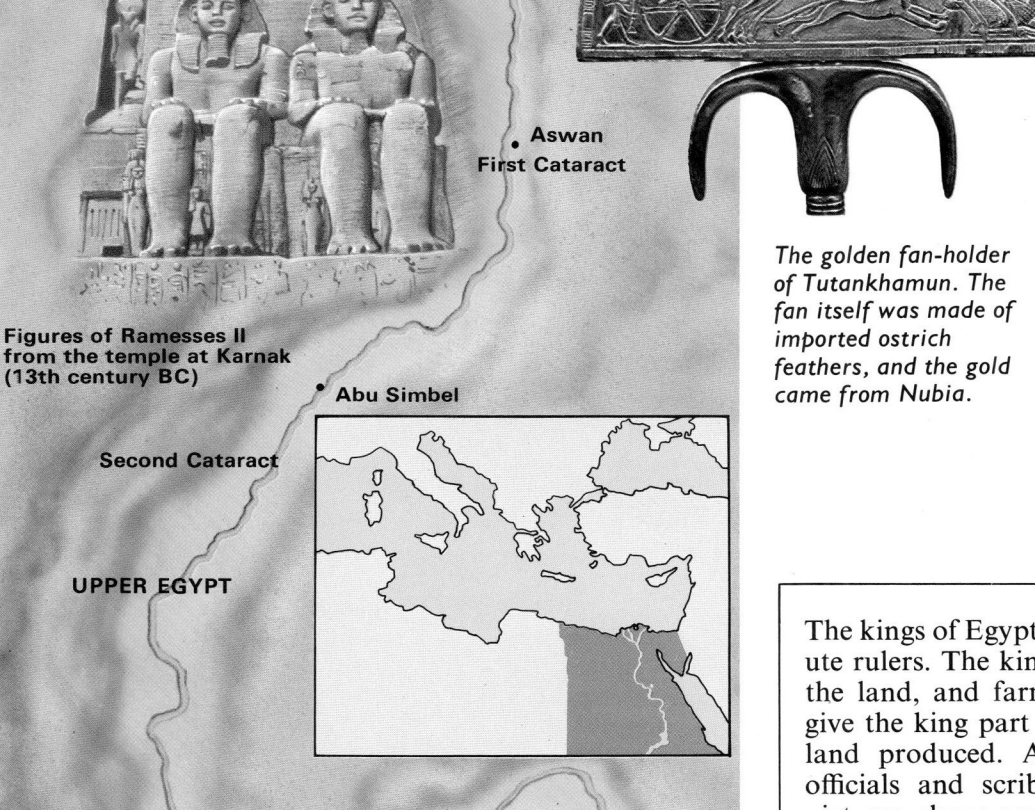

LOWER EGYPT

MEDITERRANEAN SEA

Alexandria

Giza • Cairo

The Pyramids at Giza (2000s BC)

Mask of Tutankhamun (14th century BC)

RED SEA

Tell el Amarna

Head of the pharaoh Akhnaten (14th century BC)

Thebes • Karnak • Luxor

Figures of Ramesses II from the temple at Karnak (13th century BC)

Aswan
First Cataract

Abu Simbel

Second Cataract

UPPER EGYPT

NUBIA

Nile

Egypt stretches for some 1000 kilometres north to south. In Lower Egypt, around the Delta, a few centimetres of rain fall each year. But the land watered by the Nile is astonishingly fertile.

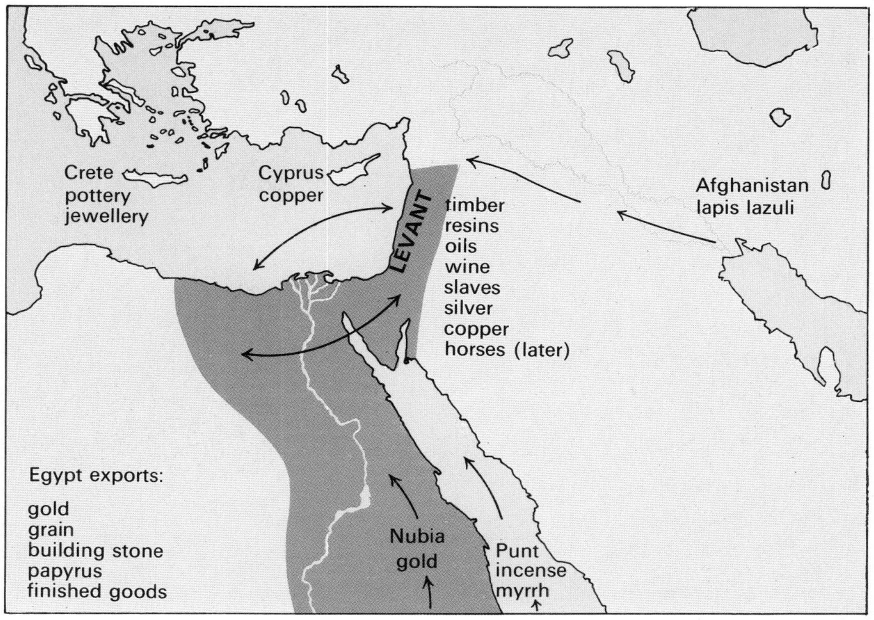

Crete
pottery
jewellery

Cyprus
copper

LEVANT

timber
resins
oils
wine
slaves
silver
copper
horses (later)

Afghanistan
lapis lazuli

Egypt exports:

gold
grain
building stone
papyrus
finished goods

Nubia
gold

Punt
incense
myrrh

Trade by land and sea linked Egypt with the rest of the Near East. There were contacts, too, with Crete. To the south, Egypt exploited the gold of Nubia and imported frankincense and myrrh from the southern land of Punt (?Somalia).

Egypt traded over a wide area. In return for grain, gold, copper, gemstones, and building stone, it imported the things that it did not have. From Lebanon came timber, resins, oils, silver, and slaves. Later, horses were imported from Syria and Anatolia, and the blue stone called lapis lazuli through Mesopotamia. Overland trade routes were protected by strong forts. During the empire, trade in Palestine and Syria was firmly controlled by Egypt. To the south, Nubia remained in Egyptian hands almost continuously for 800 years. It was Egypt's most important source of gold and slaves.

The golden fan-holder of Tutankhamun. The fan itself was made of imported ostrich feathers, and the gold came from Nubia.

The kings of Egypt were absolute rulers. The king owned all the land, and farmers had to give the king part of what the land produced. An army of officials and scribes (see the pictures above and right) had the task of fixing the exact amount due to the king from each farmer. Crops and livestock were carried off to the storehouses surrounding the royal palaces. Out of this vast tribute, the king paid his officials and provided funds for huge irrigation projects.

Cult of the Dead

The early people of the Nile Valley buried their dead in pits in the hot dry sand, which dried out the bodies and preserved them. When, later on, the dead were buried in rock tombs, the corpses decayed. So the Egyptians worked out ways of preserving (*mummifying*) them. Kings built massive pyramid tombs during their lifetime and later, to try to prevent robbery, hidden tombs were cut into cliffs in the Valley of the Kings near Thebes.

The Egyptians believed in eternal life in the Next World, and spent a lot of time preparing for it. Burial chambers were decorated with beautiful paintings and writings which recorded the dead man's life, his family and his servants, and happy days spent hunting. The Egyptians believed that in the Next World the scenes would come to life through prayer. Food and drink and little models of people were also placed there, with all the dead man's jewellery and personal equipment.

Instructions for the dead man's journey were placed in the tomb, for he faced a difficult journey across the River of Death and into the Next World before he faced Osiris, god of the dead, for the final test – the Weighing of the Heart. The dead person's heart was weighed against the Feather of Truth – a sinful, heavy heart would outweigh the feather and a dreadful monster devoured its owner; a good man would have a light heart, and would spend eternity in the Fields of the Blessed.

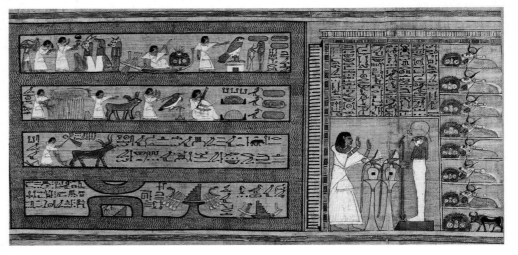

The Egyptians believed that death was only the beginning of a long journey to the Next World. The dead person would be ferried across the river to the kingdom of Osiris, the god of the dead. But there were many hazards to be overcome. To help the dead person on his journey, a book of instructions, the 'Book of the Dead', was buried in the tomb along with the body. This papyrus from the tomb of the priest Ani shows some of the stages of the journey. On the left the dead priest crosses the river; below are shown the Blessed Fields of the Next World. To the right, Ani is welcomed by Ra, the sun-god.

A prosperous farm in ancient Egypt. The fields are surrounded by irrigation ditches, one of which is being filled from a larger channel. The labourer uses a 'shaduf' to transfer the water; this is a leather bucket attached to a swivelling, counter-weighted pole. The shaduf is used in Egypt to this day. The mudbrick farmhouse has small windows set high in the wall to keep out the sun. Transport is by donkey; camels were introduced much later.

Agriculture

The farmer's year began in September, when the Nile flood, called the Inundation, began to go down, leaving a rich black silt which made the soil very fertile. Then oxen were used to drag wooden ploughs to till the soil, and by November the farmers had sown their crops – wheat for bread and fattening cattle, barley for beer, and grapes for wine. They also grew fruit and vegetables, and flax for making linen.

The farmers weeded and watered their crops, with the help of specially built irrigation canals. The crops were ready to be harvested in March and April. Then the grain was threshed and stored. The soil was so fertile that sometimes two crops could be grown before April, when the hot season began and when even the river began to dry up. So from April to June the farmers repaired the canals, dykes, and basins needed to irrigate their fields, in time for the new Inundation in June. While the land was flooded the men worked on royal projects, such as building pyramids.

Most of the land watered by the Inundation was used to grow crops. The only pasture land was in the Delta, and so in Upper Egypt cattle to be fattened for food were kept in stalls. The Egyptians also kept sheep, goats, pigs, geese, ducks, donkeys, and later, chickens. Cats and dogs were kept as pets, and horses were introduced during the Hyksos period.

TRAVEL

The river Nile was Egypt's main highway; people travelled by water wherever they could. Travel by land was hard. A rich man travelled in a chair, carried on the shoulders of servants, or very rarely by horse-drawn chariot; no other wheeled vehicles were used. Everyone else walked. Heavy loads were dragged on sledges, while smaller loads were packed into donkey panniers. Camels only began to be used in the Late Period, and the long caravans that crossed the desert before then were made up of donkeys.

Africa

The vast continent of Africa saw the rise of some of Man's earliest ancestors. Farming and the great civilization of Egypt in north Africa developed in early times. But it was only in the 4th century BC that some city-based civilizations appeared farther south and west. Farming developed in some of these areas around 1500 BC. But in many areas of Africa hunting and herding have continued until very recently to be the most satisfactory way of life. 'Civilization' (as we understand it) did not exist in many parts of Africa, but this does not mean that the people were 'primitive savages'. The complex tribal structures with their rituals, rich store of folk-tales, music, and art are proof of this.

The deserts, dense tropical forests, and mountains of Africa were all serious barriers to the spread of knowledge and ideas. In the rest of the world trade routes crossed the continents and people from one civilization met and exchanged with men from others. But Africa, apart from the Mediterranean coasts, had almost no contact with the rest of the ancient world.

Between about 15,000 and 10,000 BC Africa was much cooler than it is now. Later came warmer and wetter weather, which lasted until about 2500 BC. Rock carvings have been found in the Sahara which show that many animals lived there, providing good hunting. Lake Chad was about eight times its present size – a sign of how much more fertile the area must have been.

These Stone Age rock carvings from Algeria show a leopard and an ostrich. The place in which they are found is now part of the Sahara Desert. They are evidence of how that part of Africa has changed, for such animals could not possibly live in desert conditions.

BC	CHRONOLOGY
c30,000– 10,000	Early types of men in Africa displaced by modern hunting peoples
6000–5000	Period of rock carvings and paintings
5000–1500	Agriculture spreads southwards from early centres in Egypt and Sudan. Yam (sweet potato) cultivated in West Africa
2000	Negro herder-farmers begin to move southwards from homelands (?) south of the Sahara
c1000	Cattle- and sheep-owning peoples populate Rift Valley area of East Africa
500– AD 200	Iron-using Nok people in northern Nigeria
300	Mortarless stone structures at Zimbabwe

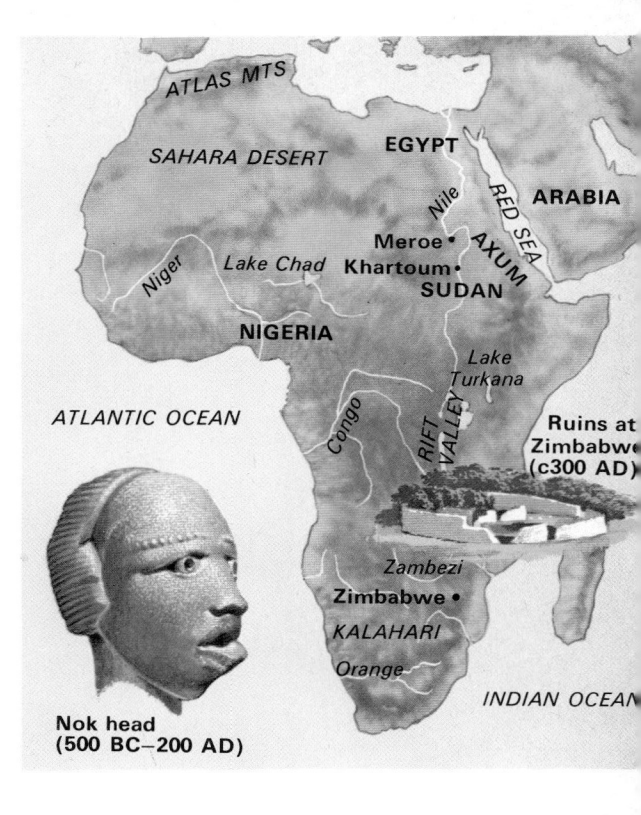

Nok head (500 BC–200 AD)

MEROE

South of Egypt lay the state of Kush. At first it was overshadowed by the greatness of Egypt itself, but after 700 BC Kush began to develop as an independent state. Meroe, which became its centre, lay at the junction of three rivers at a point where the Nile is still navigable. There were large reserves of iron ore and plenty of trees to provide fuel for smelting. Meroe was also at the end of an easy caravan route to the Red Sea. The region's wealth is shown by its stone temples, decorated with carvings. These, and a type of pyramid used for royal burials, show considerable Egyptian influence.

For a long time Meroe kept up trading contacts with the Roman empire (see page 52). At its greatest it controlled territory as far north as the First Cataract, the southern border of Egypt. But after AD 100 Meroe began to decline. In the 4th century it fell under the influence of Axum in Ethiopia, which had close connections through trade with Arabian kingdoms across the Red Sea.

In contrast, traders to the west coast of Africa had almost no contact with the people living there. The Carthaginians traded goods for gold, but left them in piles on the beach, retreating to their ships when the Africans approached!

We know very little about the early people in Africa, apart from their stone tools and some rock engravings and carvings. And there is very little evidence for the change from hunters to farmers. Wheat was cultivated in Egypt about 4400 years ago, and roughly a thousand years later goats were kept by early farmers near Khartoum. From here, agriculture spread slowly through the continent, taking 2000 years or more to move down through West Africa. We do not know just what plants were cultivated; yams were probably important in the rain forests, while some people think that rice was grown by farmers round Lake Niger perhaps as early as 1500 BC. Farther east, cattle and sheep herders may have grown millet.

The Iron Age in Africa

By far the most important widespread change in Africa was the introduction of iron – which happened south of the Sahara about 400 BC. The Nok people of northern Nigeria lived between 500 BC and 200 AD. They were skilled iron users, and also possessed specialized craftsmen who produced beautiful clay figures.

The use of iron meant that the African peoples had much greater control over their environment. Iron tools helped in timber-cutting and the clearing of new farmland. Iron weapons made men more effective warriors, and could be used for hunting. It is clear that some peoples became very powerful, like the builders of the great stone city of Zimbabwe, who moved into the area about AD 300. Although we know little about their way of life, they were skilled builders, potters, and gold miners: but they disappeared long before Europeans first began to explore the interior of Africa.

Crete and Mycenae

The Aegean Sea is an area of the Mediterranean lying between the mainland of Greece and the western coast of Anatolia. In the north-east it is linked to the Black Sea by the narrow channel of the Dardanelles, which divides Europe from Asia. The Aegean is dotted with a great number of mountainous islands. The largest of these is Crete, about 96 kilometres (60 miles) south-east of Greece itself.

The islands and coastal regions of the Aegean have much in common. All have narrow fertile plains which border the sea. Behind these strips rise steep mountains. All over the Aegean, and especially in Greece, there are deep inlets which make fine natural harbours.

The Minoans of Crete

Between 2000 and 1450 BC, the island of Crete was the most important place in the Aegean. The largest and most fertile island in the area, it was then thickly forested. Wild game, and fish from the sea, added to their crops of grain, grapes for wine, and olives, gave the islanders plenty of food.

This regular food supply gave people time to develop special crafts. As early as 4000 BC the inhabitants of Crete (called Minoans, after their legendary King Minos) used obsidian from the island of Melos to make sharp-edged blades for tools and weapons. They may have traded these with North Africa and Egypt in return for pottery. When copper came into use about 3000 BC Crete imported copper ingots from Cyprus and exported fine painted pottery, engraved stone seals, and textiles. Later, bronze objects too were made and exported.

Crete grew rich from trade between Egypt, the Aegean, and Anatolia (Asia Minor). Its seamen were among the most experienced and skilful sailors in the Mediterranean. Great centres, known as palaces, grew up at sites like Knossos, Mallia, and Phaistos. They included rooms for living in, courtyards, storehouses and workshops, and religious shrines. The palaces were centres for storing and distributing produce like grain and olive oil, and perhaps the raw materials with which craftsmen worked.

Whoever lived in these palaces controlled not only life on Crete but also a trading network spread throughout the Aegean. The fact that the palaces were not fortified shows that they felt secure from attack.

But suddenly all this came to an end. Nobody knows quite why this happened, although some people have linked it to a terrific volcanic explosion on the island of Thera in 1450 BC. The tidal wave which followed could have destroyed most of Crete's merchant ships, on which its wealth depended. Whatever happened, its great palaces were abandoned, except for Knossos, which for a short time was lived in by people from the north Aegean called the Mycenaeans.

BC	CHRONOLOGY
c6000–5000	Earliest settlements on Crete
c3000–2000	Stone-built villages on coasts in Crete. Trading contacts with Egypt, Levant, Cyclades, and Anatolia
1900–1450	Palaces built and extended. Civilization on Crete at its height. Cretan craftsmen produce their finest work
1650–1450	Greeks ('Mycenaeans') grow in power at centres such as Mycenae and Pylos
1450	Collapse of Cretan power. Knossos occupied by Mycenaeans
?1220	Troy destroyed, according to legend by mainland Greeks
c1150–1100	Collapse of Mycenaean civilization. Linear B writing disappears. Greek 'Dark Age' begins

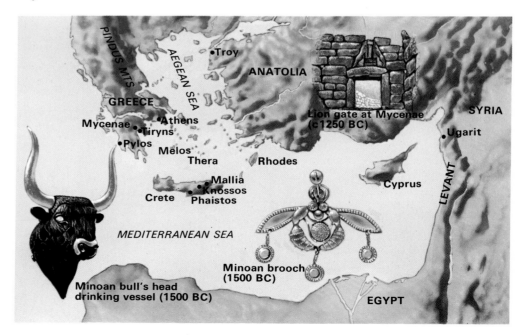

Lion gate at Mycenae (c1250 BC)

Minoan brooch (1500 BC)

Minoan bull's head drinking vessel (1500 BC)

Left: The palace of Knossos as it may have been – a great area of interconnecting buildings, courtyards, and staircases. Round grand suites of rooms were storage chambers, where rows of giant pottery vases held grain and oil, and the workshops of skilled craftsmen.

Below: The 'throne room' at the palace of Knossos; both the throne and the elaborate wall paintings (which have been heavily restored) date from the Mycenaean occupation of Crete, but earlier wall paintings have been found in many Minoan buildings.

The Mycenaeans

While the trading empire of Crete was at its most important, Greek-speaking peoples were living in cities on the coasts of mainland Greece. Historians call these people 'Mycenaeans' after the site of Mycenae, where the first traces of them were found.

The Mycenaeans' cities usually grew up near the coasts, for two main reasons. Here, the most fertile land lay in a narrow coastal strip fringing the rugged mountains inland; while the mountains made land travel more difficult than travel by sea. Strong, fortified towns were built which dominated the fertile countryside around. Each town had a central strongpoint (citadel), such as a steep hill. In time of war the whole population could retreat to the safety of the city.

Who were the Mycenaeans? This is a problem. It is possible that people from Anatolia may have moved into Greece about 1900 BC; but Mycenaean civilization also had many links with the earlier culture of Greece and probably developed gradually between 1900 BC and 1600 BC. By 1600 BC the Mycenaeans were trading in the Aegean, although Crete was still the most important trading power.

After the fall of Crete, Mycenaean trading stations and settlements were set up over a wide area, from Sicily and south Italy to the coast of Syria. There were close links, too, with Troy, at the mouth of the Black Sea, which was a rich grain-growing area.

But after 1300 BC trade in the eastern Mediterranean suddenly declined, for reasons we do not know. This must have been a time of growing dangers, for the citadels at Mycenae, Tiryns, and Athens were now strengthened with massive walls of stone. About 1200 BC, the whole region went through a time of violent upheaval. Centres in Greece, Asia Minor and the Near East were sacked and burned. At this time small bands of pirates and adventurers (who may be connected with the 'Sea Peoples' of Egyptian texts) were raiding in the southeast Mediterranean. They may have played a part in the area's decline, or they may have joined up during the economic crisis it caused. Whatever the reasons, a period of chaos followed in which the Bronze-Age civilization of the Mycenaeans disappeared to be remembered only dimly in legends.

Right: A mask of beaten gold discovered in a royal tomb at Mycenae. Large numbers of gold and silver objects were buried with the Mycenaean rulers, and their workmanship shows links with the Near East and Crete.

A bronze Mycenaean dagger inlaid with a scene of a lion hunt. The tall shields carried by the hunters are like those described in Homer's 'Iliad', a 9th-century poem telling of the legendary destruction of Troy.

The circle of graves at the palace of Mycenae. The palace commanded great stretches of the surrounding country; it was heavily fortified and had its own water supply.

The World in 1500 BC

In the south-east Mediterranean Egypt is an imperial and trading power of enormous wealth; its trading contacts include the Minoans of Crete and the Mycenaeans of mainland Greece. In Mesopotamia the Kassites are in control of Babylonia while Assyria is just a vassal of the neighbouring state of Mitanni. The Hittites control Anatolia (Asia Minor). Bronze spreads through the Old World. In China the first historical period, the Shang dynasty, begins; in northern Europe the last great *megalithic* structures (made of huge stone slabs) are erected while in the Americas cultivation spreads, and the first ceremonial centres are built in Peru.

Copper mining and working in the Austrian Alps, in the 12th century BC. There were no explosives to make tunnels. Instead, a fire was lit against the rock and when this was hot, cold water was thrown against it to make it split. When the fires had been put out miners hacked the ore from the cracked rock with bronze picks. Outside the mine it was crushed and washed, then smelted in furnaces heated with wood from the forests around.

3 Northern Europe and Scandinavia Early Bronze Age. Smiths produce fine, often highly decorated weapons and ornaments.

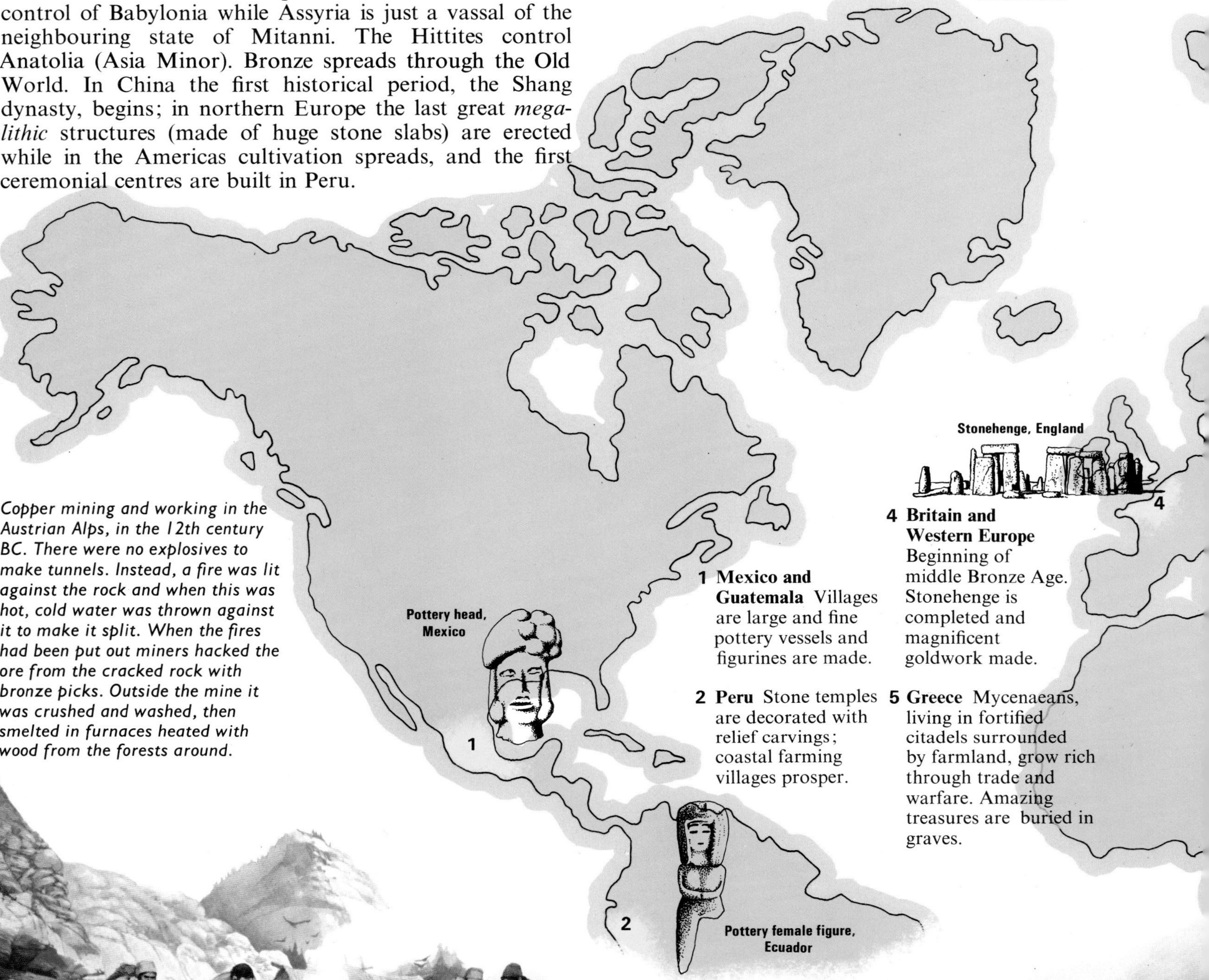

Stonehenge, England

4 Britain and Western Europe Beginning of middle Bronze Age. Stonehenge is completed and magnificent goldwork made.

Pottery head, Mexico

1 Mexico and Guatemala Villages are large and fine pottery vessels and figurines are made.

2 Peru Stone temples are decorated with relief carvings; coastal farming villages prosper.

5 Greece Mycenaeans, living in fortified citadels surrounded by farmland, grow rich through trade and warfare. Amazing treasures are buried in graves.

Pottery female figure, Ecuador

By 1500 BC the first Indian civilization, based in the Indus Valley, had disappeared. Excavation of its great centres at Harappa and Mohenjo-Daro has shown how highly organized it was. On the right is a reconstruction of the huge state granary at Mohenjo-Daro to which farmers brought their grain.

Rock carving, Sweden

Hittite god, Anatolia

3

7 Anatolia Hittites rule a huge empire centred on Hattusa (Boghazköy), using horse-drawn war chariots.

11 China Beginning of Shang dynasty. Oracle bones show writing. Fine bronzes are made and chariots used in war.

Bronze bull's head, Mycenae

5

7

8

9

Chinese bronze vessel

11

10 India The Indus Valley civilization, with its magnificently planned cities, has broken up around 1750; as yet nothing comparable has taken its place.

The gold sarcophagus of Tutankhamun. He was a minor boy pharaoh who reigned in the 14th century BC. His tomb, in the Valley of the Kings near Thebes, contained astonishing treasures underlining the immense wealth of Egypt at this time.

Indus Valley head

6

10

Tutankhamun model, Egypt

8 Crete Luxurious palaces like Knossos witness a rich civilization based on trading agricultural produce. This ends about 1450 perhaps through a nearby volcanic eruption. For about 50 years Mycenaeans occupy Knossos until overcome by unknown disaster there.

6 Egypt The New Kingdom; Egypt becomes an imperial power. Pharaohs are buried in the Valley of the Kings, including Tutankhamun, a minor boy-pharaoh whose magnificent grave-goods demonstrate Egypt's riches.

9 Mesopotamia Kassites rule over Babylonia; they trade with Egypt, receiving gold in return for lapis lazuli.

India

The subcontinent of India is a great triangle of land jutting southwards from the mainland of Asia. To the north-east towers the immense range of the Himalaya mountains. In the north-west high mountain passes lead to Afghanistan and on to Iran. Much of India is a high tableland, the Deccan, surrounded by mountains. Between the northern mountains and the Deccan lie vast fertile river plains. In the east is the plain of the Ganges; and in the west that of the Indus and its four tributaries, known as the Punjab, or Land of the Five Rivers.

India is a land of great local variations of climate and vegetation, but as a whole, it is very dry for seven months of the year. Most of the rain falls between June and September, carried by a warm wind from the south-west which is called the monsoon.

At Mohenjo-Daro there was a complicated system of water and drainage tanks and channels. This building, known as the Great Bath, may have played some part in religious ceremonies.

The Indus Civilization

The first civilization of India grew up in the fertile Indus valley about 2500 BC. Until the 20th century nothing was known of it, apart from vague legends written down by the people who lived in this area many centuries later on. Now archaeologists have found the remains of two great cities, Mohenjo-Daro and Harappa, and more than a hundred lesser towns and villages.

The Indus valley people depended on a large-scale system of dams and canals to control the fierce flooding of the river Indus, and to make the best use of its waters in the dry season. In this way large tracts of land could be farmed and used to feed a large settled population. Farmers grew wheat and barley, and were the first to cultivate cotton. They tended herds of cattle and buffalo, and probably knew how to tame elephants for heavy work. In the cities, craftsmen worked in gold and copper imported from Afghanistan and Rajasthan, made fine pottery, and were expert carvers of ivory. Trade over land and sea linked the Indus valley with Iran, Mesopotamia, and even the eastern Mediterranean. However, despite all its wealth, and its splendid administration, the Indus civilization collapsed about 1750 BC. Some cities were destroyed, and the population slaughtered.

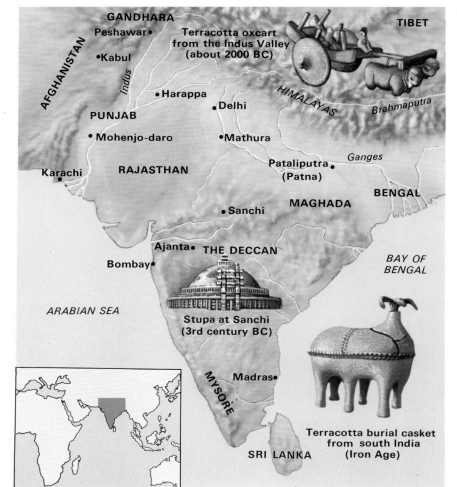

Terracotta oxcart from the Indus Valley (about 2000 BC)

Stupa at Sanchi (3rd century BC)

Terracotta burial casket from south India (Iron Age)

Below: A carved stone seal showing a domesticated buffalo, and writing which no one can now read. Seals like these would have been used by administrators. Bottom: Indian civilization grew up in river plains like this. The land is fertile, but flooding is always a danger.

BC	CHRONOLOGY
c2500–1750	Indus Valley civilization
c1500–1000	Early 'Aryan' (Vedic) period in Ganges Valley
c600	Early cities in Ganges Valley
563	Birth of the Buddha
533	Persians invade India
c550–342	Maghada empire in north-east India
326	Alexander the Great in India
324–187	Mauryan empire
100s–	
cAD 200	Andhras dominate central India
187–75	Shunga dynasty in northern India
AD	
15–300s	Kushans rule northern India
320–535	Guptas rule northern India

THE INDUS CITIES

The two great centres of the Indus valley civilization were Mohenjo-Daro and Harappa – about 600 kilometres (375 miles) apart. In these cities lived administrators, merchants, craftsmen, and shopkeepers. They were fed by the farmers of the surrounding countryside, who brought grain in two-wheeled ox-carts to store in the huge city granaries. Both cities were laid out in a pattern of rectangular blocks divided by wide roads. Within the blocks were brick houses, opening into central courtyards. The houses were separated by narrow lanes, with rows of shops.

Each city was dominated by a raised, fortified platform on which were built huge mudbrick storehouses for grain, assembly houses and, perhaps, temples. There were excellent drainage systems, and a large number of public wells provided a constant water supply.

The polished stone capital of one of the many pillars put up at the orders of the great emperor Ashoka in the 3rd century BC.

The Ganges Valley

Over several hundred years new peoples from the west, often called the Aryans, moved into the Indus area. They may have been responsible for the final breakdown of the Indus civilization about 1750 BC.

The descendants of the Aryans slowly spread eastwards into the Ganges Valley. They spoke an Indo-European language distantly related to Greek, Hittite, and Persian. By about 1000 BC, men in the Ganges Valley had learned how to smelt iron ore and make iron tools and weapons.

By the 6th century BC great cities had grown up on the sites of the Iron-Age villages. They were built of brick and stone and were surrounded by high walls and moats. Like the independent city-states of Greece, these cities controlled the farmland around them. The Ganges cities were often at war, but gradually one centre, Maghada, became more powerful than its neighbours. It ruled a huge kingdom in the north-east. Later this came under the rule of the Mauryan dynasty, which eventually united nearly all of India. The greatest of the Mauryan emperors was Ashoka (273–232 BC) who brought peace and order to his huge empire. But within 50 years of his death, his empire had broken up.

The Indus Valley civilization lasted from about 2500 to 1750 BC. After its decline, 'Aryan' peoples moved westwards into the Ganges Valley (1500–1000).

By AD 150, India was divided into three main empires: the Kushan, Kshatrapa, and Andhra states. They gave way to the Gupta empire (320–535) based in Maghada.

The Andhras

One of the former subject tribes, the Andhras, grew steadily in power in the Deccan. By the 2nd century AD they dominated central India from coast to coast. They built splendid stupas – Buddhist monuments – decorated with wonderful stone carvings. They also carved ivory most skilfully, and some of their carvings reached Pompeii in southern Italy. At this time Hindu culture developed in South India and Sri Lanka, which were mostly free from foreign influences.

After invasions by Persia (533 BC) and Alexander (327), the Mauryan dynasty (324–187) gained control of much of India. It was greatest under Ashoka (273–232).

INVADERS FROM THE WEST

Northern India is hemmed in by mountains. To the east are the almost impassable Himalayas, but to the west high passes lead to Afghanistan and Persia. This means that north-west India has always been more closely in contact with the western world than with East Asia.

In 533 BC King Cyrus II of Persia advanced into the Punjab. Two centuries later Alexander the Great of Greece invaded north-west India. His Greek soldiers were soon driven out, but early in the 2nd century Greeks from the kingdom of Bactria occupied north India as far east as Pataliputra. Next came Scythians (known as Shakas), and then the Kushans from central Asia who conquered northern and much of middle India. Through these passes, too, the White Huns invaded in the 5th century AD.

This 'reliquary' (container for sacred objects) comes from the province of Gandhara, in the north-west of India. It was briefly part of Alexander's empire, but Greek influence lasted long after Alexander's death. Four centuries later, when this reliquary was made, the figures on the sides still show a mixture of Indian and Greek styles. The Gandharan craftsmen were skilled in stone carving, and also famous workers in gold and precious stones. Here, the stones are rubies.

Anatolia

Anatolia, also called Asia Minor, is a broad peninsula jutting westwards from the continent of Asia itself. To the north lies the Black Sea, to the south the easternmost part of the Mediterranean. At the entrance to the Black Sea are the narrow straits of the Bosporus and the Dardanelles. Here Asia comes closest to the continent of Europe. Because of this, Anatolia has always been the main link between east and west.

Anatolia is a very varied region. The coasts have a Mediterranean climate – warm dry summers, and cool wet winters. But in the mountains inland the winters are very cold and the summers extremely hot. At the centre is a high tableland, the Anatolian plateau: to the south-east, the high Taurus mountains divide Anatolia from Syria.

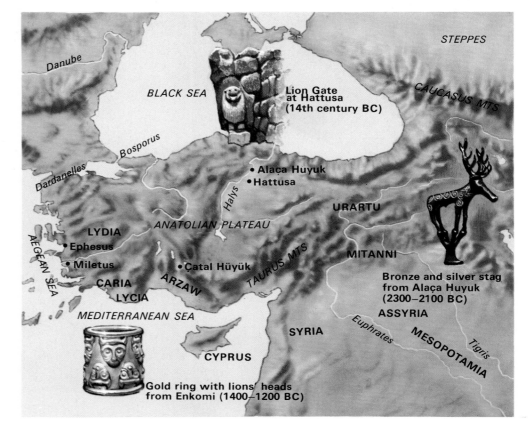

Early Farmers

The history of Anatolia is confusing because of the different peoples who lived there. Its steep mountain ranges made travel difficult, so that developments in one area could not spread easily to others. Until the Hittites emerged in about 1700 BC, we can get only brief glimpses of events in the area.

From about 8000 BC it is clear that farming was carried on in settled upland villages in eastern Anatolia. Cattle-raising, however, did not begin until nearly 6000 BC. As well as farming, there was an ancient trade in Anatolian obsidian and Syrian flint. These were rocks used to make tools and weapons. Later on, trade in other natural resources – such as copper and possibly silver – grew up. Between 3000 and 2000 BC, bronze working was highly developed in Anatolia.

Anatolia was rich in copper, gold, silver, and iron and in the skills to work them. It had strong trade contacts with the rest of the Near East. But the mountainous terrain was a barrier to easy conquest.

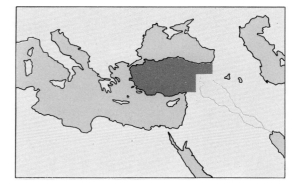

CATAL HÜYÜK

Between 6000 and 5000 BC more than 5000 people lived in Çatal Hüyük in central Anatolia. They grew wheat, barley, and vegetables. They kept sheep and goats, and hunted aurochs (wild cattle), deer, and wild pigs. Çatal Hüyük's prosperity was only partly due to agriculture. It probably controlled the trade in obsidian, a hard, volcanic glass which its craftsmen turned into sharp-bladed tools and weapons. Other craftsmen were expert woodworkers and weavers.

Çatal Hüyük is one of the earliest towns we know of, not just in Anatolia but anywhere in the world. But it did not lead to the development of a true city-based civilization. As yet, no one knows why this was.

Houses in Çatal Hüyük were built in terraces round courtyards; there were no streets, and they were entered across the flat roofs and down ladders. The houses were built of mud bricks round a timber frame. Many of these houses may have served as shrines. Their walls were decorated with paintings of vultures and headless men, and with modelled animal figures. These included leopards, which may have been kept as sacred pets.

This view, looking towards the ancient Hittite capital of Hattusa, shows the fertile land which lies among the mountains in this region.

A gold drinking vessel or rhyton made by Thracian craftsmen in the 3rd century BC. The Thracians lived in south-east Europe and parts of Anatolia. They built no great cities, but their chiefs lived in fortified settlements, surrounded by warriors. They acknowledged a single king who was also their high priest. Their craftsmen were famous for their beautiful and skilled metalwork.

BC	CHRONOLOGY
3000–2000	Early Bronze Age in Anatolia. Links with Aegean and North Syria
2000s	City-states recognize a 'great prince' as overlord
c1650–1460	Hittite Old Kingdom. Their armies using horse-drawn chariots conquer North Syria and invade Mesopotamia
1460–1180	Hittite Empire phase
c1200	Hittites overwhelmed by Phrygians from the north. Hittite provinces in North Syria survive until the 8th century
c1000	Greek cities founded on Aegean coast. They later colonize Black Sea coasts
c900	Western Anatolia divided into small kingdoms, among them Lydia which expands to include much of central Anatolia
545	Cyrus the Great of Persia conquers Lydia and dominates Greek cities on the western Anatolian coasts

The Hittites

About 2000 BC, a number of Indo-European peoples moved into Anatolia, probably from the north-west. Among them were the Hittites, who eventually settled in Anatolia. Little is known of this period – but by 1700 BC the Hittites ruled an area around their capital at Hattusa.

The Hittites expanded westwards across Anatolia, and southwards into Syria. This brought them into conflict with the Egyptian empire. After a series of wars, Egypt recognized the Hittite empire as *the* great power in the north.

In the east, the Hurrian state of Mitanni and later the Assyrians threatened the Hittites. In the west, the state of Arzawa and the Ahhiyawa (who are thought by some to be Mycenaean Greeks) were challenging Hittite control of the trade routes. In 1200 the whole area was thrown into confusion by the attacks of the 'Sea Peoples'. The Hittites in Anatolia disappeared from history. Only in Syria did Hittite provinces survive. They lasted for another 500 years before falling to the Assyrians in the 8th century BC.

New Rulers

After the collapse of Hittite power, Anatolia was occupied first by the Phrygians, and then in about 700 BC by the Cimmerians. At the same time the small princedoms of Lydia, Lycia, and Caria, which had been dominated by the Hittites grew more powerful. The Lydians were rich in river gold and in the 6th century their ruler, Croesus, was legendary for his wealth. But he was defeated by Cyrus the Great of Persia, and Anatolia became part of the Persian empire.

Urartu

In the confusion following the fall of the Hittites, new states were set up. Urartu (the biblical Ararat) was made up of several smaller kingdoms. Its lands reached from eastern Anatolia north-eastwards to the Steppes of southern Russia. Urartian kings built fortified cities to protect them from raids by the Scyths, who were nomads from the Steppes. Huge engineering works brought water to irrigate the fields. Urartian farmers raised cattle, and grew a wide variety of crops. Linen and cloth weaving were major industries.

For a long time Urartu acted as a strong check against the expansion of the Assyrian empire. But in the 6th century BC, it finally fell to the Medes and Scyths, who had joined together.

GREEK CITIES OF ASIA

On the coasts of the Aegean Sea and on islands off the west coast of Asia Minor there were Greek cities, which had been settled in the 10th century. On the coasts of the Black Sea, too, were Greek colonies, founded in the 8th and 7th centuries. They grew grain in the fertile lands around. Some of the cities, like Miletus and Ephesus, became rich and powerful. They had close links with one another through trade and their common language and traditions. But their independence was often threatened by powerful rulers in Asia Minor – first the Lydians, and then the Persians.

The Greek Cities

Greece is a rugged, mountainous peninsula running south-east from the mainland of Europe into the Mediterranean. The summers are hot and dry, the winters cool and rainy. Today the mountains are bare and rocky, but in Ancient Greece they were covered in thick forest.

In those days Greece was more fertile than it is now. Even so, the fertile areas were cut off from one another by the mountains. There were small pockets of farmland between the sea and the mountains, and in the bottoms of narrow, winding mountain valleys. The best land of all lay in central Greece, between Athens and Thebes, and farther south in the interior of the Peloponnese, the southern peninsula of Greece.

The mountains formed barriers that made overland travel difficult, so small, isolated states grew up. These depended very much on the sea for communication with the outside world. As time went on and populations grew, they relied more and more upon trade, for large numbers of people could not be supported by farming alone.

The Acropolis at Athens. Originally the defensive strongpoint of the city, this rocky outcrop became a symbol of Athenian power and prestige. By the 5th century BC the Acropolis was a glittering complex of shrines and temples. The most famous was the Parthenon, sacred to Athene, the city's patron goddess.

The Rise of the City-States

The strong citadels of the Mycenaeans, their society, and culture finally collapsed by about 1100 BC. For 200 years most of Greece became a land of scattered farming settlements, ruled by local chieftains. The pattern of population changed and the number of people was much smaller: more people were living in Attica, Euboea, and the Cyclades and some people from mainland Greece settled in Cyprus.

By the 10th century BC, Greeks had settled on most of the Aegean islands and the coasts of Anatolia (Asia Minor) with citadels (*poleis*) to protect their farmland. These settlements traded with the Near East.

They were later the homes of some of the greatest Greek thinkers and scientists.

The Greeks probably learned alphabetic writing from the Phoenicians. As this spread, it helped all Greeks to realize that they shared the same language and heritage. Contacts were renewed between the eastern Greeks and the mainland.

Between 800 and 700 BC, growing populations forced the many Greek states (particularly the eastern ones) to settle new areas. They planted colonies first on the fertile shores of the Black Sea, then far to the west in Sicily and southern Italy. By 550 BC there were hundreds of Greek settlements, from Spain to the Black Sea.

The Greek world about 550 BC. From Spain to the Black Sea, Greek colonists founded new cities. They spread Greek language and culture far from the tiny states of mainland Greece.

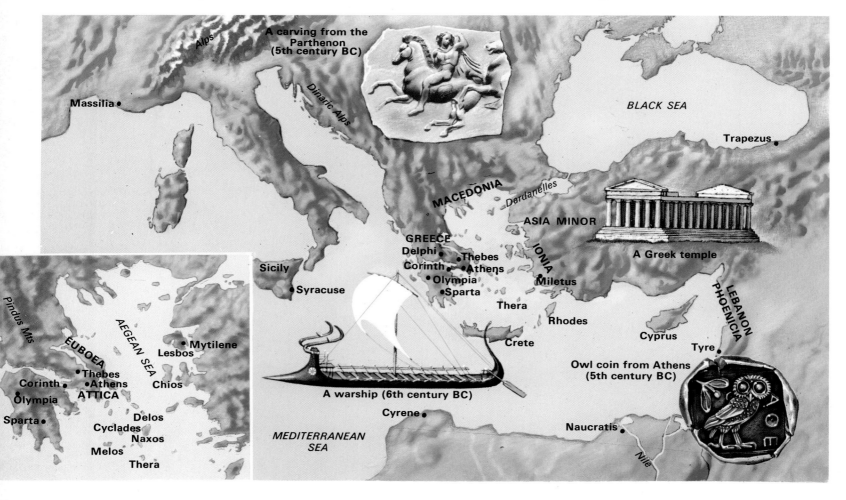

A carving from the Parthenon (5th century BC)

Alps

Dinaric Alps

Massilia

BLACK SEA

Trapezus

MACEDONIA

Dardanelles

ASIA MINOR

GREECE

Delphi

Thebes

Corinth

Athens

IONIA

Olympia

Sparta

Miletus

A Greek temple

Sicily

Syracuse

Thera

Rhodes

LEBANON

PHOENICIA

Crete

Cyprus

Tyre

Owl coin from Athens (5th century BC)

A warship (6th century BC)

Naucratis

Cyrene

MEDITERRANEAN SEA

Nile

Pindus Mts

EUBOEA

AEGEAN SEA

Mytilene

Lesbos

Corinth

Thebes

Athens

Chios

ATTICA

Olympia

Sparta

Delos

Cyclades

Naxos

Melos

Thera

Harvesting olives – an Athenian black-figure vase. The Athenians exported olive oil to pay for foreign grain.

A typical Greek house of the 5th century BC. The street entrance leads through a passage into an open courtyard. The rooms are simply furnished; even well-to-do citizens frowned on luxury.

BC	CHRONOLOGY
c1000	Greek settlers colonize coasts of Anatolia
850–750	Independent city-states grow up in mainland Greece. Corinth is especially powerful
850–550	Eastern and mainland Greeks set up colonies from the Black Sea to Spain
546	Persia begins to take over Greek cities in Anatolia
?507	Athenian democracy begins
490–479	Persia twice unsuccessfully invades mainland Greece
477–405	Athenian navy dominates Aegean. Athens's Golden Age
431–404	Peloponnesian war between Athens and Sparta ends in Athens's defeat. Sparta rules Greece
356–338	Warfare between Greek states allows Philip of Macedon to master Greece

TRADE AND TYRANTS

By the 6th century BC, mainland Greece was at the centre of trade between the western and eastern Mediterranean. The city of Corinth, on the narrow strip or isthmus of land connecting northern and southern Greece, became very powerful. The Corinthians built a slipway, the *diolkos*, across the isthmus. Large ships were dragged across it by teams of oxen – saving several days sailing around the southern tip of Greece.

The Greeks built merchant ships to carry their trade goods. They also built warships with which they controlled the eastern Mediterranean. When the Persians invaded Greece the Athenian navy played the greatest part in their defeat. This made Athens the powerful leader of an alliance of Greek islands.

A procession of Spartan warriors, from a metal vessel. All male Spartan citizens were trained from childhood to become soldiers. Their toughness and courage were legendary. This cup dates from the 6th century BC.

Athens v. Sparta

There was always great rivalry between the city-states of Greece. This was partly to do with the cities' own pride in themselves. The worst rivalry of all was between Athens and Sparta in the 5th century. The two could not have been more different. Athens was a democracy – all citizens could vote to say how they should be governed. Sparta was a military state. Every male citizen had to spend his life serving in the army: all work was done by serfs, called *helots*, who were treated cruelly. The Athenians despised the Spartans who seemed barbarians to them: the Spartans thought the Athenians dangerous revolutionaries. In 431 the two cities and their allies went to war – a long, bitter struggle that left Greece weak and divided. In the end Sparta was victorious. The Spartans became leaders of the Greek states, but there were constant revolts. Eventually King Philip of Macedon, to the north, moved in to take control of the country.

A bust of Pericles, who led Athens in the middle of the 5th century BC and made it into the most magnificent city in Greece.

The theatre at Delphi, site of the great Greek shrine to the god Apollo. The Greeks believed that at certain places like this the gods came into close contact with the world of men. To all Greeks, the importance of these sacred sites was far above political differences. At festivals like the four-yearly Games to Zeus at Olympia, even Greek states at war joined together to pay homage to the gods.

The World in 500 BC

By now the first great centres of civilization, Mesopotamia and Egypt, have declined; both have fallen to the Persians, who in less than a century build up an empire from Egypt in the west to India in the east. As they move north, the Persians come into conflict with the Greek city states, which dominate the eastern Mediterranean. Most important of these are the warlike Sparta, and Athens, famous for its art and democracy. The use of iron has spread through much of the old world.

3 Central and Northern Europe From 700 BC the iron-using Hallstatt culture has spread out from Austria; hill forts are surrounded by farmland. In 450 the Celtic La Tène culture develops, with its delicate metalwork and splendid gold ornaments.

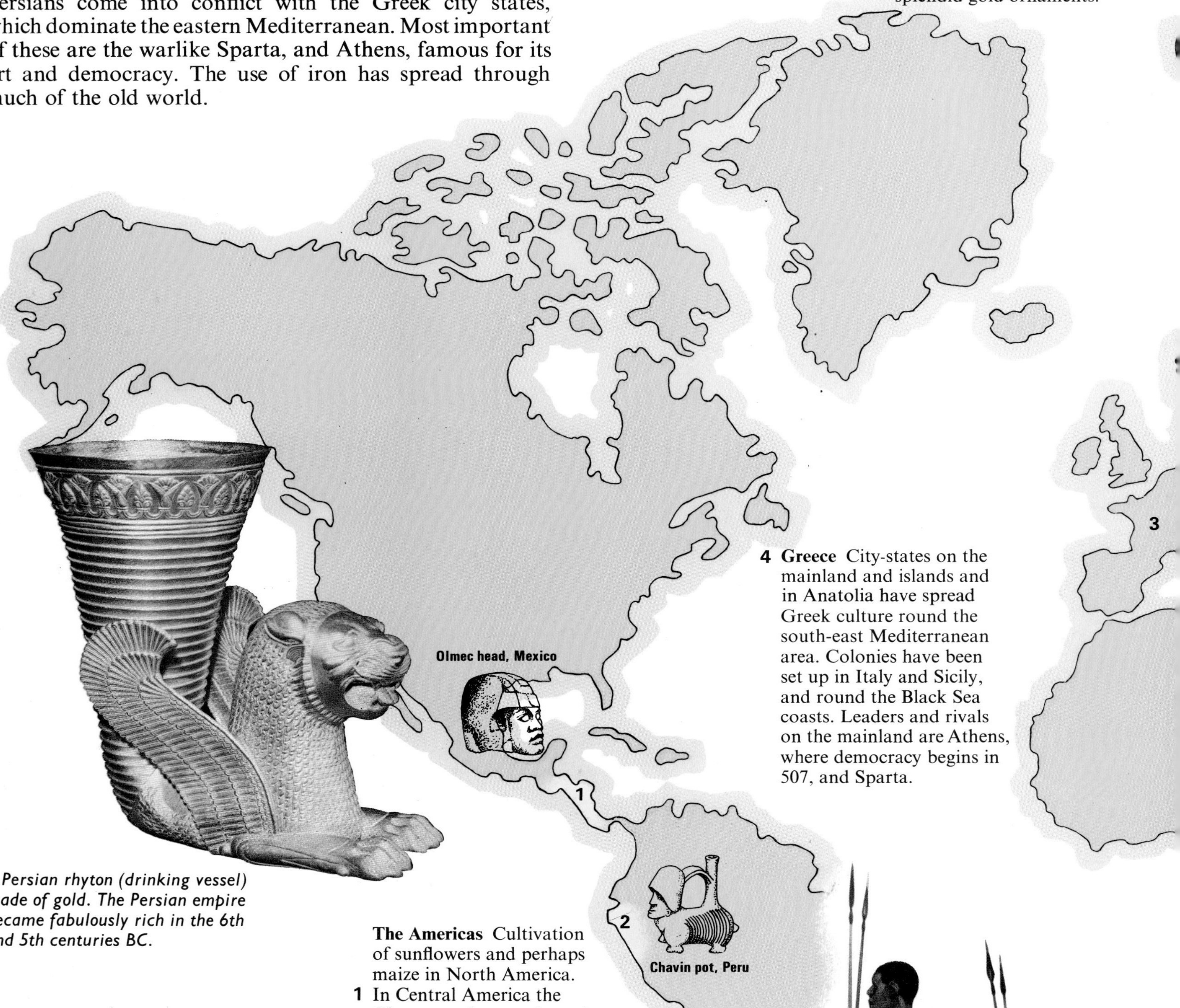

Olmec head, Mexico

4 Greece City-states on the mainland and islands and in Anatolia have spread Greek culture round the south-east Mediterranean area. Colonies have been set up in Italy and Sicily, and round the Black Sea coasts. Leaders and rivals on the mainland are Athens, where democracy begins in 507, and Sparta.

A Persian rhyton (drinking vessel) made of gold. The Persian empire became fabulously rich in the 6th and 5th centuries BC.

Chavin pot, Peru

The Americas Cultivation of sunflowers and perhaps maize in North America.
1 In Central America the Olmec people near the end of their dominance; in Peru the Chavin people
2 make fine pots in human and animal shapes.

Carthaginians trading with Africans on the island they called 'Cerne', off the coast of Senegal. The exchange of trade goods was carried on through some kind of agreed sign language.

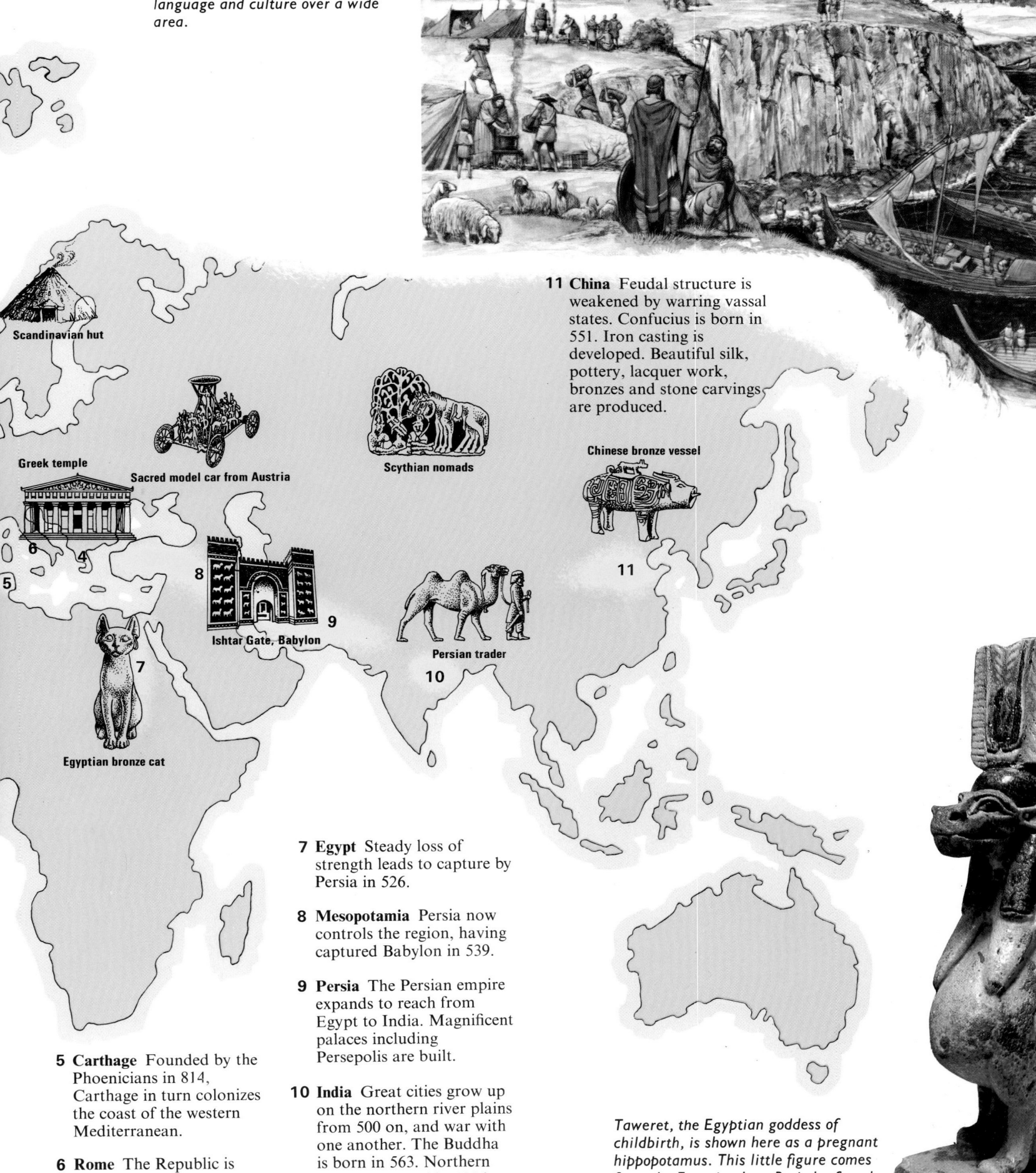

An expedition of Greeks founds a new colony. Between 750 and 550 BC over-population in mainland Greece forced people to search for new places to live. A string of new Greek cities along the coasts of the Mediterranean spread Greek language and culture over a wide area.

Scandinavian hut

Greek temple

Sacred model car from Austria

Scythian nomads

11 China Feudal structure is weakened by warring vassal states. Confucius is born in 551. Iron casting is developed. Beautiful silk, pottery, lacquer work, bronzes and stone carvings are produced.

Chinese bronze vessel

Ishtar Gate, Babylon

Persian trader

Egyptian bronze cat

7 Egypt Steady loss of strength leads to capture by Persia in 526.

8 Mesopotamia Persia now controls the region, having captured Babylon in 539.

9 Persia The Persian empire expands to reach from Egypt to India. Magnificent palaces including Persepolis are built.

10 India Great cities grow up on the northern river plains from 500 on, and war with one another. The Buddha is born in 563. Northern India is invaded in 533 by the Persians.

5 Carthage Founded by the Phoenicians in 814, Carthage in turn colonizes the coast of the western Mediterranean.

6 Rome The Republic is founded in 509 after the Etruscan kings are expelled.

Taweret, the Egyptian goddess of childbirth, is shown here as a pregnant hippopotamus. This little figure comes from the Egyptian Late Period, after the 7th century BC.

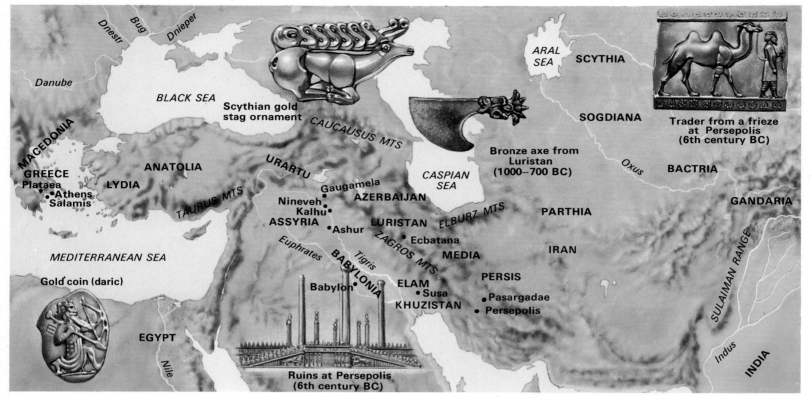

Scythian gold stag ornament

Bronze axe from Luristan (1000–700 BC)

Trader from a frieze at Persepolis (6th century BC)

Gold coin (daric)

Ruins at Persepolis (6th century BC)

The Persian Empire

The land of Persia, or Iran, stretches eastwards from the Zagros mountains almost to northern India. Much of it is a vast, high desert tableland, surrounded by mountains. But around the borders are more fertile regions: Azerbaijan and the Caspian plain in the north, and the wide Khuzistan plain to the south.

Iran has a great range of climate and in many places rainfall is irregular. As a result many groups followed a nomadic way of life, as some still do. During the scorching heat of summer the peoples of Iran took their herds to the pastures of the cool, fertile upland valleys of the mountains. Here they grew wheat, barley, vines, figs, and pomegranates. The lower slopes of the mountains were thickly wooded with wild almond, walnut, and pistachio trees.

Throughout its history Iran was often invaded by nomadic peoples. Some came through the Elburz mountains, east of the Caspian Sea. Others, like the Medes and Persians, entered Iran through the Caucasus mountains in the north-west.

By the 9th century BC the most powerful group in Iran was the Medes with their Persian vassals. Their kingdom, Media, lay in the north-west: to the west and north it was hemmed in by the strong states of Assyria and Urartu.

In 612 BC the Medes, together with the Babylonians, captured Nineveh, Ashur, and Kalhu. The Assyrian empire came to an end and its vast territories were divided between the Medes and the Babylonians.

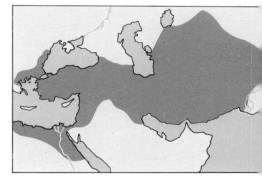

The splendour surrounding the Persian kings drew craftsmen and precious metals from all over the empire. This leaping winged ibex, of partly gilded silver, originally formed the handle of a bowl. It was made in the 4th century BC.

BC	CHRONOLOGY
3000s	Elamite civilization in south-west Iran
1300s	Medes and Persians move into Iran
600	Cyaxares, king of the Medes, destroys Assyria
549	Persians under Cyrus II the Great defeat Medes and conquer Lydia
539	Babylon falls to Persians
533	Cyrus II invades India
526	Cambyses conquers Egypt
490–479	Persians under Darius and Xerxes unsuccessfully invade Greece
331	Alexander of Macedon conquers the Persian empire

Elam was the region between south-west Persia and south Mesopotamia. It developed its own civilization around 3000 BC. Little is known of its history. Left: King Teumann of Elam and his son Tammaritu fleeing from the conquering Assyrians in the 7th century BC.

Right: The ruins of the palace at Pasargadae, in south Persia. It was built by Cyrus the Great. Like all the great Persian palaces, it stood on a vast man-made terrace, and two grand staircases led up to it.

The Rise of the Persians

In about 550 BC the king of the Persians, Cyrus the Great, overthrew his Median overlords. From now on the Persians ruled over Iran. Cyrus captured Babylon and gained control of the whole of the former Babylonian empire – virtually all of western Asia was now under Persian rule. The next two kings, Cambyses and Darius, extended Persian rule to Egypt in the south and to the borders of India in the east. Darius organized his vast empire into provinces, ruled by *satraps* (governors), and linked by a network of superb roads.

In spite of revolts in the provinces and plots in the palaces, Persian kings continued to hold most of their empire. The exception was Egypt, which successfully revolted against Artaxerxes II (404–359 BC). Artaxerxes III (359–338 BC) was able to recapture Egypt. But before he could turn his attention to the problem of Greece, he was poisoned. After two years of confusion, Darius III came to the throne. Before he could establish himself, he was faced with the invasion of Greeks and Macedonians led by Alexander the Great. Alexander defeated Darius's army at the great battle of Gaugamela in Mesopotamia; Darius fled, but was soon murdered by one of his own governors. With his death, the Persian empire came to an end.

Right: Persian kings commanded a personal guard of 10,000 soldiers, like these archers from the palace at Susa.

THE SCYTHIANS

The Persian empire included a number of nomad peoples. Among them were Scyths or Scythians, who had moved west from the Asian steppes in about the 8th century, and had established themselves in south Russia, Armenia, and north Iran. They moved swiftly between grazing grounds, the men on horseback and the women and children in large felt-roofed waggons. They took with them cushions and wall-hangings of brightly decorated felt. Some had ornaments and vessels of beautifully worked gold, like the one in the picture on the left. Much of what we know comes from Scythian tombs at Pazyryk in Siberia, which were preserved by the freezing climate. Men and women were buried with their possessions, the men's bodies tattooed with animal designs.

Alexander the Great from a mosaic found at Pompeii in southern Italy.

Alexander and After

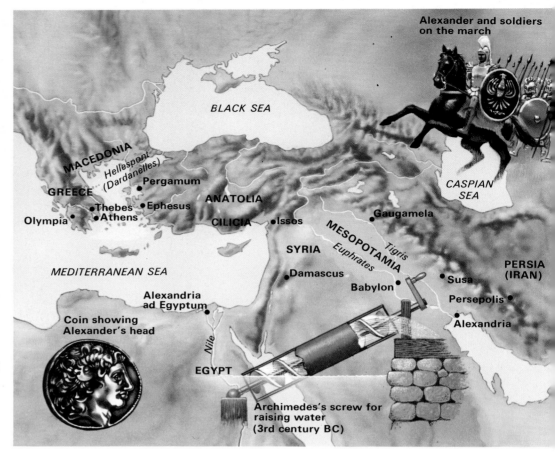

Alexander and soldiers on the march

BLACK SEA

MACEDONIA
Hellespont (Dardanelles)
GREECE
Thebes • Pergamum
Olympia • Athens • Ephesus
ANATOLIA
CILICIA
• Issos
Gaugamela
MESOPOTAMIA
SYRIA
Tigris
Euphrates
CASPIAN SEA
PERSIA (IRAN)
Damascus
Babylon
Susa
Persepolis •
MEDITERRANEAN SEA
Alexandria ad Egyptum
Coin showing Alexander's head
Alexandria
Nile
EGYPT
Archimedes's screw for raising water (3rd century BC)

Alexander of Macedon was one of the greatest generals the world has ever seen. In ten years of constant fighting he conquered the Persian empire and spread Greek domination as far as north-west India. His great conquests mark an important point in history. Before him, the greatest advances in civilization were made in Asia – from the beginnings of farming to the first cities and empires. With Alexander the first European-controlled empire was born. From now on Europe, still largely undeveloped, began to be the centre of progress.

The ruins of the Philippeum at Olympia. This building was commissioned by Philip of Macedon to celebrate his victory over the Greeks at Khaironeia in 338 BC. The victory gave Philip control of Greece. Many Greeks despised Philip, thinking his kingdom was barely civilized.

Philip of Macedon died in 336 BC. In a few years he had taken advantage of the quarrels between the Greek city-states to bring them under his power. But at his death the royal treasury was empty.

Philip's son Alexander was only 20 years old, and barely 150 centimetres (5 feet) tall. The Greeks thought him a mere boy, and soon the city of Thebes rebelled against him. Swiftly Alexander and his army attacked the city and captured it, killing the population. After this, no other Greek city dared to revolt.

Alexander still had to find money. For a long time Greeks had envied the fabulous wealth of the Persian empire. They saw too that the empire was weak. Alexander brought together a huge army of 24,000 Greek and Macedonian troops. He made sure that the army was backed up by special battalions of engineers and medical staff.

In 334 BC, Alexander led his army across the Hellespont into Anatolia. Always fighting at the head of his troops, Alexander won a number of small battles before meeting the main Persian army, under Darius III, at Issos. Darius's army was beaten, and he fled, leaving the way open to Syria and Egypt. After conquering Egypt, Alexander turned north and east into the heart of the Persian empire.

BC	CHRONOLOGY
336	Alexander inherits throne of Macedon. He becomes undisputed master of Greece
334	Alexander with a Greek and Macedonian army invades Anatolia
333	Alexander defeats Persians under Darius III at Issos
331	Battle of Gaugamela. Alexander now controls Persian empire
330–325	Alexander conquers provinces in eastern Iran and north-west India
323	Alexander dies in Babylon
323–319	Struggles between Alexander's generals and their heirs for his empire
188	Syria submits to Rome
168	Macedonia becomes a Roman province
146	Romans combine Greek cities with province of Macedonia
133	Pergamum bequeathed to Rome
65–63	Pompey annexes Cilicia and Lydia for Rome
30	Egypt becomes a Roman province

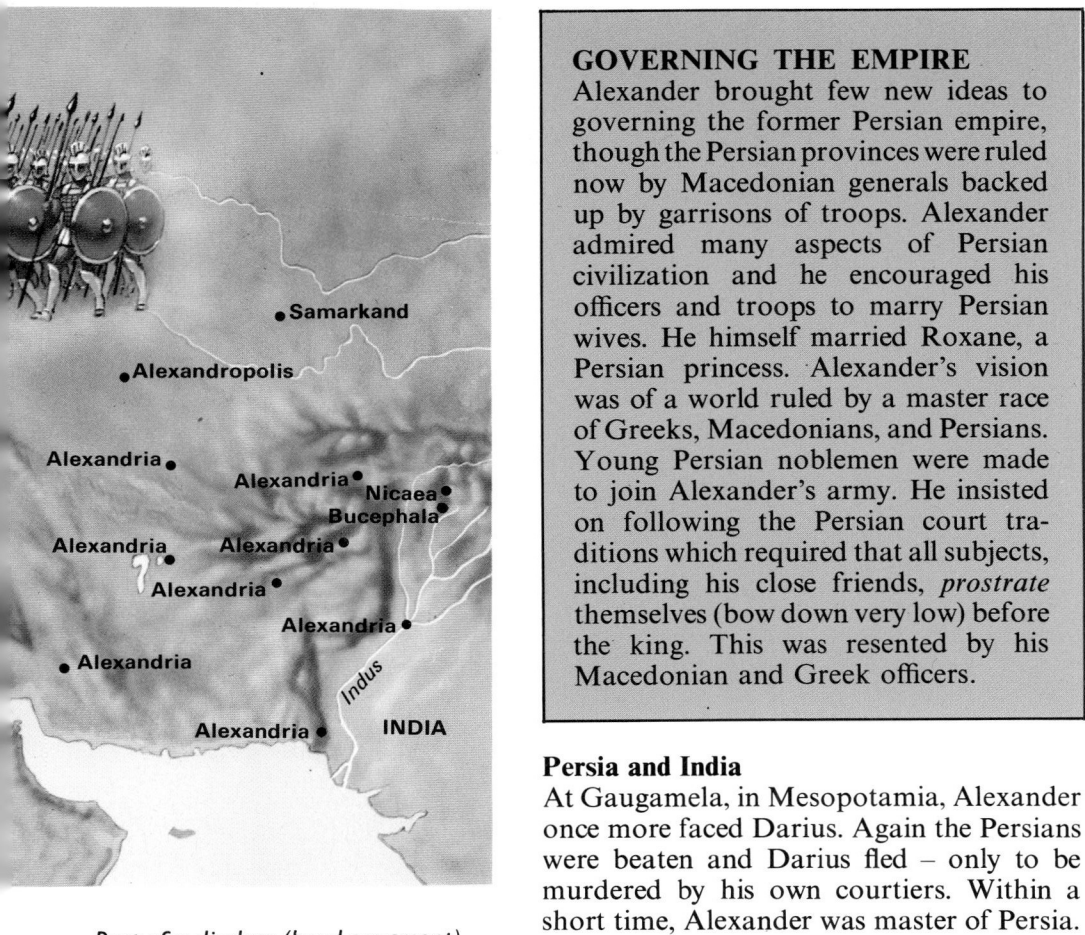

Part of a diadem (head ornament) made in Hellenistic times. It is in the form of a Herakleian knot. This knot was used to show the descent of the family of Alexander the Great from the legendary hero Herakles (Hercules), and it often appears in Hellenistic ornaments.

GOVERNING THE EMPIRE

Alexander brought few new ideas to governing the former Persian empire, though the Persian provinces were ruled now by Macedonian generals backed up by garrisons of troops. Alexander admired many aspects of Persian civilization and he encouraged his officers and troops to marry Persian wives. He himself married Roxane, a Persian princess. Alexander's vision was of a world ruled by a master race of Greeks, Macedonians, and Persians. Young Persian noblemen were made to join Alexander's army. He insisted on following the Persian court traditions which required that all subjects, including his close friends, *prostrate* themselves (bow down very low) before the king. This was resented by his Macedonian and Greek officers.

Persia and India

At Gaugamela, in Mesopotamia, Alexander once more faced Darius. Again the Persians were beaten and Darius fled – only to be murdered by his own courtiers. Within a short time, Alexander was master of Persia.

Not content with his victory, Alexander led his army on into north-west India. Only when his battle-weary troops refused to go farther did Alexander return. He was planning new campaigns of conquest when he died, perhaps from poison, in Babylon in 323 BC.

When Alexander died his son by Roxane was too young to rule and was soon murdered. His empire was divided up between his generals (above). His shieldbearer Seleukos and his descendants ruled over a vast federation of provinces, stretching eastwards to the lands of the Indian ruler Chandragupta. Ptolemy and his descendants ruled over Egypt. Anatolia was ruled by Antigonus. These divisions were arrived at only after bitter warfare.

The map above shows the Hellenistic world in about 180 BC. The Seleukids had lost part of their lands to the Parthians and Bactrians. The Antigonids now ruled only over Macedonia in northern Greece. Anatolia was divided into a number of small kingdoms, the most important of which was Pergamum. These fought among themselves and were soon to be taken over by Rome, the rising Mediterranean power.

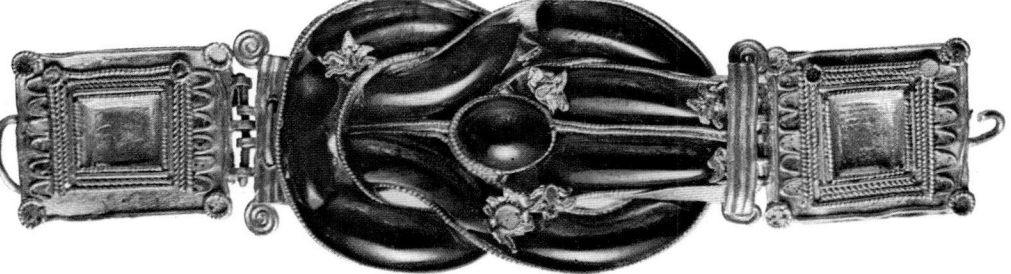

Ruins of the ancient Greek city of Ephesus, in Anatolia. The eastern Greek cities, liberated from the Persians by Alexander in 333 BC, rose in renewed splendour. The vast wealth of the defeated Persian empire was used for magnificent temples, theatres, and public buildings.

ALEXANDRIA

The greatest of the Hellenistic cities was Alexandria in Egypt, founded by Alexander the Great in 322, and chosen by Ptolemy as his capital. He enlarged the harbour and built the Pharos lighthouse, one of the wonders of the ancient world. Alexandria became a naval base and trading port – the largest and richest Greek city in the world. Its library contained about 700,000 rolls of papyrus and parchment by the 1st century BC, and Alexandria became a centre for poets, writers, philosophers, and perhaps above all for scientists. Euclid wrote his geometry book, Eratosthenes showed that the world was round, and Archimedes and Hero invented machines including a steam turbine. Alexandria was captured by Muslim Arabs in the 7th century AD. Some of them became skilled scientists and learned much from the writings of the ancient Greeks.

The Bible Lands

The biblical land of Canaan, the 'land of milk and honey', was an area about 160 kilometres (99 miles) wide, running north to south along the east coast of the Mediterranean. In modern times the region includes the states of Israel, Jordan, Lebanon, and part of Syria. The area made up of Israel and Jordan is often known as Palestine.

This is an area of great variety, divided down the middle by high mountains and the deep valley of the river Jordan which is the lowest point on the Earth's surface. In the west lies a narrow, fertile coastal strip. To the east and south a jumble of rocky hills and valleys merges into arid desert wilderness.

Farming began about 8000 BC, and the land was rich enough to grow wheat, vines, and olives. Mudbrick towns grew up around local water sources. However, away from the coast, fertile areas were scattered and separated by stretches of semi-desert. As a result no large-scale food production developed as it did in Egypt or Mesopotamia. But the region was always important. It formed a route between Africa and Asia, along which the armies of many empires marched. It was the crossroads of trade routes from east to west and north to south. It possessed natural resources, like the cedars of Lebanon, which attracted the great powers of Egypt, Mesopotamia, and the Hittites. Desert nomads like the Amorites, Aramaeans, and later the Israelites could move in from the east. In the west there were contacts with seafaring traders from Cyprus, Anatolia (Asia Minor), and the Aegean.

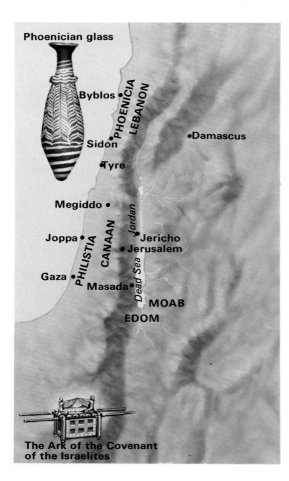

Phoenician glass

The Ark of the Covenant of the Israelites

BC	CHRONOLOGY
8000–2000	Farming carried on. Large towns such as Jericho grow up. Later small independent kingdoms emerge
1200	After disruption by raiders much of the region is settled by Israelites, Aramaeans, and Philistines
995	The Israelite King David builds a fortified capital at Jerusalem
722–539	Assyrians, then Babylonians, control region; Jerusalem falls 597 and many exiled to Babylon; from 539 region passes to Persia and exiles return, known from now on as Jews
331–63	Palestine and Syria become part of Alexander's Hellenistic empire and at last fall to Rome

The hill fortress of Masada, near the Dead Sea, was the last stronghold of Jews when they revolted against Roman rule from AD 66 to 73.

The top map shows the land of Canaan. The map above shows its key position in the Near East, connecting Egypt, Mesopotamia, and Anatolia.

Shifting Peoples

About 2000 BC the land was invaded by Semitic desert peoples, the Amorites. The area now had close links with Egypt through trade. Later, Hyksos ('foreign rulers') from Palestine drove into Egypt and controlled much of it until they were finally expelled about 1550 BC. Soon after 1468 BC Palestine and Syria became part of an Egyptian empire. About 1200 BC, Canaanite civilization was destroyed by raiding bands and was followed by the settlement of Israelites and Aramaeans. By 1150 BC the Israelites were farming in the hills west of the Jordan, while the Aramaeans were established in northern Syria, Lebanon, and the area round Damascus. The Philistines, related to the earlier raiders, were occupying the coastal strip from Gaza to Joppa.

Part of an Assyrian relief showing cedar logs from the forests of Lebanon being floated downstream to be used in an Assyrian palace.

The Phoenicians

During the 12th century many coastal cities were destroyed. The few that survived were strung along the narrow, mountainous strip of coast that we call the Lebanon: the main cities were the ancient ports of Byblos, Tyre, and Sidon. The Greeks called the people of Lebanon 'Phoenicians'.

Their greatest natural resource was the great cedar forests of the high mountain slopes. For 2000 years cedar timber had been traded through the port of Byblos. Now the Phoenicians built up a great fleet of merchant ships. Exploratory expeditions were probably sent as far as Britain and the west coast of Africa. In the western Mediterranean the Phoenicians founded many colonies, including Carthage on the coast of Africa, and Cadiz in Spain.

To the Lebanon came linen from Egypt, and silver, iron, lead, and tin from Spain and Sardinia. From Africa came ivory, slaves, gold, silver, apes, and peacocks. Canaan provided grain, honey, and oils: south-east Anatolia exported horses and mules. Over-land routes linked Phoenicia to the Red Sea, Arabia, and Mesopotamia.

But the wealth of the Phoenicians was not only based on buying and selling these goods. They were also famous for their craftsmen, who turned raw materials into finished items which were exported over a wide area from Italy to Mesopotamia. Weavers wove cloth from wool imported from Syria. The cloth, together with Egyptian linen, was dyed with the famous 'Tyrian purple'. This was a dye made from a kind of shellfish. Phoenician metalsmiths worked in bronze, iron, silver, and gold.

At their greatest, the Phoenicians con-trolled a vast network of trading colonies from Cyprus to Spain. Even after the Lebanon fell under the domination of great empires, the cities themselves remained wealthy. In the west, the Phoenician empire of Carthage survived to compete with the growing power of Rome.

The ivory carvings of Syria and the Lebanon were much prized in the Near East. The lion from Phoenicia (left) wears a wig and chest ornament in the Egyptian style. It was made in the 9th or 8th century BC. The ivory figure of a man (below) comes from North Syria, and dates from the 10th or 9th century.

THE BIBLE AND HISTORY

The Israelites were wandering herds-men from the edge of the desert west of Mesopotamia. From time to time, small changes in climate seriously affected the grazing on the desert's rim. When this happened some desert peoples moved into the settled, fertile areas of Mesopotamia, Syria, and Palestine. One such migration may have been that of a small group led by Abraham, moving from North Syria into Canaan about 2000 BC.

A few centuries later a similar nomadic group (according to the Old Testament, descended from Abraham) moved to Egypt in search of new pastures for their flocks. It was not unusual for Egyptians to allow nomadic tribes to graze their flocks on unwanted pasture in the 'Land of Goshen', east of the Delta. Generations later, some of these people had become slaves. Under the leadership of Moses they fled into the wilderness of the Sinai Desert, where they joined other similar people. After wandering for many years they reached Canaan (about 1200 BC), and established themselves in villages among the hills and valleys west of the Jordan. From now on we can speak of them as the 'Israelites'.

After many battles the Israelites defeated the neighbouring peoples, and under King David they set up a secure kingdom with a capital at Jerusalem. But under his grandson the Israelites divided into two hostile states, Israel and Judah. From now on control of the area changed from one great power to another as empires rose and fell. In AD 70 its Roman rulers destroyed Jerusalem after a revolt; in 135, after another uprising, they drove the Jews out of Palestine.

China

The first great civilization of the Far East grew up in China, and spread so widely that it strongly influenced almost all the other Far Eastern countries. This was a civilization that grew up in isolation, for China is cut off from the western world by the mountains of Tibet to the west, and by the Gobi Desert and Manchurian Plain in the north-west and north.

Three great river systems dominate China. In the south is the Si-kiang or West River. Here the climate is tropical and rice is grown all through the year. But this area is rather cut off from the rest of China by mountains that, though not very high, are difficult to cross. Through central China runs the Yangtze River. Here summers are hot and moist, though the short winters can be very cold. And to the north is the Hwang-ho or Yellow River. Its name comes from the fine yellow soil which covers the highlands through which the river flows, and which it carries down to spread over its flood plain. Here the summer rains are slight and unreliable, while the winters are long, dry, and bitterly cold. North-west winds from the Gobi Desert swirl the soil into dust storms. The Yellow River often floods disastrously, drowning thousands of people and sweeping away villages and crops. But the yellow soil is so fertile that it was along the Yellow River that China's first civilization grew up.

Kneeling pottery figure (3rd century BC)

Bronze flying horse (2nd century AD)

This red lacquer bowl dates from the Chou period. Lacquer was the sap of an oak tree, which became very hard and black when left in a damp place. The Chinese built up layer upon layer of lacquer on a thin core of wood or cloth, and often coloured it and decorated it with gold or silver.

Below: In the north China highlands the yellow soil may be 100 metres (about 325 feet) thick. When dry it blows off in dust storms, but when wet it becomes very fertile. From very early times the Chinese joined together in elaborate irrigation schemes.

BC	CHRONOLOGY
c5000	Village farming communities in the Hwang-ho (Yellow River) Valley
c1500	Bronze-working begins in An-yang region. Shang dynasty rules an empire with its main capital at An-yang
1027	Chou people from west China defeat Shang and establish a feudal dynasty, ruling many vassal states
771	Chou move capital to Loyang
c700–500	Vassal states grow in power and Chou are weakened
660	Nomad barbarians ravage north Honan
551	Confucius born
481–221	Warring States period
256–221	State of Ch'in emerges victorious. First Ch'in emperor, Shih Huang-ti, unites China and consolidates Great Wall
206	Ch'in dynasty collapses
206– AD 220	Han dynasty
50–AD 50	Buddhism introduced from India
AD 166	Marcus Aurelius sends embassy to China
220–587	Six Dynasties period

A gilded bronze incense burner dating from the Han dynasty. Chinese bronze workers were very skilled in casting elaborate vessels. They used moulds fitted together from a large number of pieces, which allowed them to cover their work with decorations. Bronzes were often gilded and inlaid or lacquered.

Unbroken Traditions

All over the ancient world great civilizations grew up and then died away. But Chinese civilization was never destroyed; instead, it developed without a break until the 20th century. From time to time invaders conquered and settled parts of the north, but they did not change the Chinese way of life; instead, they learned it themselves.

The earliest villages and towns grew up on the banks of the Yellow River and its tributaries. The water was used to irrigate the yellow soil and make it fertile. Cities were surrounded by walls of *hang-t'u* (stamped earth), built up layer by layer and pounded so solid that many are still standing today. The first period of Chinese history we know about is the time when the Shang dynasty ruled in the Yellow River area, from about 1500 BC on. Later dynasties spread Chinese rule and ways of life west and south. At its greatest the Chinese empire stretched from North Korea in the east, far west into Central Asia.

The Chinese empire was governed by a vast number of efficient civil servants, some employed by the central government and some by local government. In the name of the emperor, they controlled all aspects of every day life. Weights and measures, laws and taxes were made the same all over the empire. Only this sort of strong central rule could hold such a vast area together.

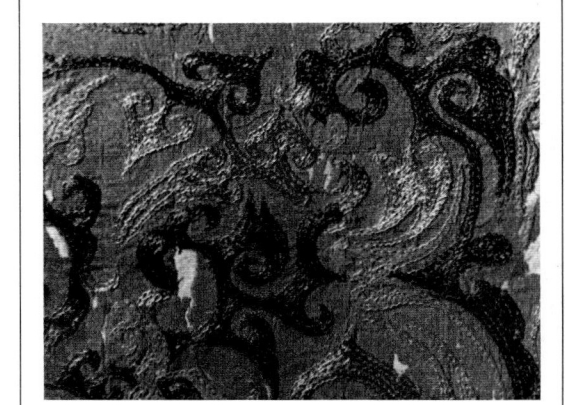

Silk was China's most famous export. For centuries only the Chinese knew how to get silk from silkworm cocoons. This piece of embroidered silk dates from the Han dynasty.

TRAVEL

China's main link with the rest of the world was the Silk Road. This led from China, through Sinkiang, Turkestan, and Bactria, and then to Persia and Syria. Along this road long caravans of camels carried Chinese goods, especially silk, to the west. China imported little in return except for jade from central Asia and pearls from the south.

Within China itself, the main highways were the rivers and the many canals, which were used by countless boats. Special roads were built for moving armies and their supplies. Government officials were allowed to travel along the imperial highways, but most people used rough tracks.

AGRICULTURE

One of the Han dynasty emperors said 'the world is based on agriculture' and most people in ancient China worked on the land. In the north wheat, millet, and barley were the most important crops; farther south, rice was grown. Orchards of fruit trees were planted around the villages. Pigs and sheep were kept, but few cows – the Chinese have never liked milk or any of its products, and cattle were mainly used to pull carts. Hens and geese were important. Tea and cotton, which are both so common in China today, were not cultivated in ancient times, but hemp, from which cloth was made, was an important crop.

A model of a house, dating from the Han dynasty. Much of our knowledge of ancient China comes from such pottery figures and models found in tombs, showing animals, houses, farms, and servants.

Hunting was a popular pastime in ancient China. In Shang times young men set out in chariots; cheetahs, falcons and hounds were used to chase the prey.

47

Europe under the Romans

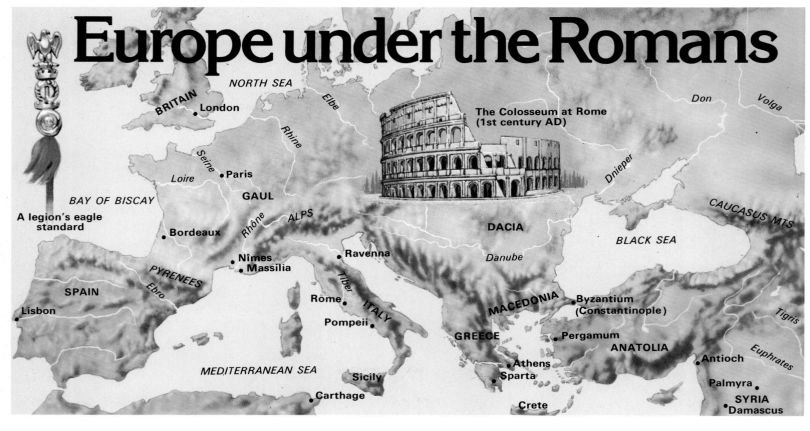

NORTH SEA
BRITAIN
London
Elbe
Don
Volga
Rhine
Seine
Loire
Paris
GAUL
BAY OF BISCAY
A legion's eagle standard
Bordeaux
Rhône
ALPS
Nîmes
Massilia
Ravenna
PYRENEES
Ebro
SPAIN
Tiber
Rome
ITALY
Lisbon
Pompeii
Carthage
Sicily
MEDITERRANEAN SEA
Crete
The Colosseum at Rome (1st century AD)
Dnieper
CAUCASUS MTS
DACIA
Danube
BLACK SEA
MACEDONIA
Byzantium (Constantinople)
GREECE
Pergamum
ANATOLIA
Athens
Sparta
Antioch
Euphrates
Tigris
Palmyra
SYRIA
Damascus

Until 250 BC, trade in the Mediterranean was controlled by Phoenician and Greek colonies on the coasts. At the same time, however, a new power was growing in Italy – the city-state of Rome. Between 250 and 30 BC Rome gained control of the whole Mediterranean region, the Near East, and a large part of western Europe. How did this happen?

Rome's rise to power was based on the position of Italy itself. As trade developed in the western Mediterranean, Italy became an important link between west and east. Just as important were the resources of Italy, which was very fertile, although not yet developed. In the south, Greek colonies grew rich: but central and northern Italy were mountainous regions, inhabited by many warring tribes. Only when Rome had united Italy under its leadership could the full value of Italy's position and resources be seen.

The Growth of Rome

Rome began, perhaps in the 800s BC, as a group of hilltop settlements which overlooked the river Tiber, and beyond that the fertile plain of Latium. For several hundred years the area was dominated by the Etruscans of north central Italy. In 509 BC the native Romans rejected the rule of their Etruscan king, Tarquinius, and set up a republic. Instead of the hated king, they elected two magistrates, the consuls, to rule them. The new republic was a community of farmers, who cultivated the fertile countryside around the city.

BC	CHRONOLOGY
900s	Rise of Etruscans in North Italy
753	Traditional date of founding of Rome
509	Founding of Roman republic
343–275	Rome becomes dominant in Italy
264–201	Rome defeats Carthage and gains first overseas provinces
133–60	Aristocratic and popular parties struggle for power
59–52	Caesar conquers Gaul
49–44	Dictatorship of Caesar
44	Caesar assassinated; after conflict with Mark Antony Caesar's nephew Octavian (Augustus) gains power and becomes emperor
AD	
286	Diocletian divides empire into west and east
476	After barbarians overrun France, Spain, and Italy, last western emperor is deposed

javelins THE ARMY
helmet
pickaxe
mess tin
shield

Whenever the need arose, the Roman farmers made tough, disciplined troops, always ready to fight in defence of their lands. Over the next 500 years they had to fight many enemies. By 266 BC Rome was the leading power in Italy. Then came two bitter wars with the North African city of Carthage, Rome's greatest rival in the western Mediterranean. Once again, Rome was victorious.

The next challenge came from the wealthy Greek kingdoms of Anatolia, Macedonia and Syria. By 80 BC these had come under Roman rule. Then, in 59 BC, Rome turned north. An ambitious Roman aristocrat, Julius Caesar, invaded Celtic Europe, which the Romans called Gaul. Caesar conquered all of Europe west of the Rhine. During the next hundred years the Romans won even more territory, including Britain: Rome ruled everything west of the Rhine and Danube rivers except Scotland and Ireland.

Rome's empire was won by the steadiness of the well-disciplined Roman troops. At first, the army was made up of farmer-citizens. But when the army was fighting abroad for long periods, the farms suffered from neglect. Under the consul Marius, just before 100 BC, the army was changed into a permanent, paid force. The biggest unit of the army was the legion; it was made up of 6000 (later 4000) men, divided into ten cohorts. The cohort was made up of six centuries, each numbering 100 troops. Marius's soldiers were issued with standard equipment (see left). As well as fighting, they had to build fortifications, roads, and bridges.

Administering the Empire

Rome's greatest gifts to its empire were orderly government and technical knowledge. The Romans knew that they could not rule their vast empire by force of arms alone. In return for loyalty to Rome, the Romans allowed conquered peoples to keep their own customs and, to a certain extent, to govern themselves. To Europe, still a wilderness, the Romans brought their skills as builders, engineers, and farmers. They built towns and cities, connected by excellent roads. Roman landowners developed organized farming in Europe, draining marshes and clearing woodland to make fertile farmland. Trade and craftsmanship began to flourish, and came to rival even those of Italy itself. The Celtic people of Europe were encouraged to take part in all this. As time went on they settled peacefully into a Romanized way of life.

Roman occupation of southern Gaul brought a steady development of trade and agriculture. The Pont du Gard (above) was built to bring water to Nîmes (Nemausus), one of the richest towns of Roman Gaul.

The frontiers of the Roman empire were defended by a chain of walls and forts. Hadrian's Wall in the north of England was built between 122 and 136. It was part of a defensive zone many kilometres deep.

In Rome itself, luxury and poverty lived close together. Wealthy citizens occupied large ground-floor apartments in blocks ('insulae'). But the upper floors were overcrowded with poor families.

Heroic Societies

The peoples of central, northern, and western Europe did not develop cities until long after south-east Europe and the Near East. When Egypt and Crete were at their most powerful and glorious, Stonehenge was just being given its final form.

Before Roman occupation, the peoples of Europe formed what are called 'heroic societies'. Tribal chiefs and their warriors lived in hill forts surrounded by timber-framed ramparts. They were supported by farmers who worked the country around, herding animals or growing grain. Specialist metal-workers travelled through the countryside, skilfully producing goods first of bronze and later of iron. In the 5th century BC the Greeks described all the inhabitants of western Europe, from Spain to the Danube, as *Keltoi* – from which we get our term Celts.

The Celts soon accepted Roman ways. But east and north of the river Rhine were other tribes, together known as 'barbarians'. They constantly raided and threatened the Roman frontier, and eventually broke through to cause the empire's downfall.

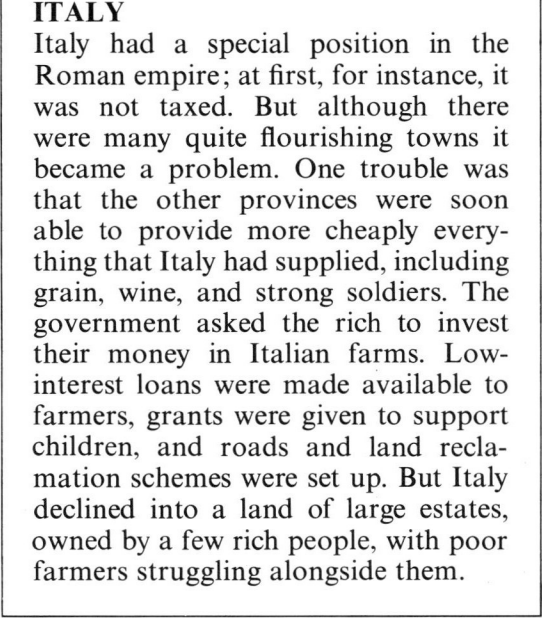

ITALY

Italy had a special position in the Roman empire; at first, for instance, it was not taxed. But although there were many quite flourishing towns it became a problem. One trouble was that the other provinces were soon able to provide more cheaply everything that Italy had supplied, including grain, wine, and strong soldiers. The government asked the rich to invest their money in Italian farms. Low-interest loans were made available to farmers, grants were given to support children, and roads and land reclamation schemes were set up. But Italy declined into a land of large estates, owned by a few rich people, with poor farmers struggling alongside them.

The World in AD 117

In AD 117 the Roman empire reaches its greatest extent, from Britain in the north and Spain in the west, eastwards to Mesopotamia. In the eastern Mediterranean the influence of Greece is still very strong, with Greek culture admired by everyone and Greek the language of educated people. But to the north the empire is threatened by barbarians who are starting to shift southwards and westwards. In China under the Han dynasty patterns of life become established that will last for 1800 years, while in Central America the Maya civilization emerges.

3 Central and Northern Europe west of the Rhine and Danube become rich through trade and accept Roman ways. Across these rivers 'barbarian' tribes resist attempts at conquest.

1 America In Central America small city states compete for power. In the low-lying forests the Maya build ceremonial centres and use their own form of hieroglyphic writing. On **2** the Peruvian coast pottery and textiles are produced.

Celtic bronze head

Pottery figures, Mexico

4 North Africa prospers under the Romans; vines, grain, and olives are grown on irrigated land and cities are built.

This Celtic bronze shield probably dates from the 1st century AD. It was found in the river Thames at Battersea in London. The central design includes four owl faces, simplified into a decorative pattern.

Below: A Roman military camp was a miniature city. Built to a standardized pattern, it had special areas set aside for the high command, ordinary soldiers, stabling, and so on. Familiar patterns and routines in unfamiliar surroundings helped keep up the spirits and effectiveness of Roman forces far from home.

Pottery fragment, Peru

5 Eastern Mediterranean Rome allows the old cities to keep their way of life; the area is united by its Greek-derived culture and the Greek language. The Jews refuse to be governed by Rome and Judaea is eventually annihilated in AD 130.

6 Egypt Under Roman rule a 'river of grain' flows from Egypt to Rome, while Alexandria is a centre of trade and learning.

The Han emperors of China governed their huge territory with the help of an army of civil servants. These officials were treated with great respect. All parts of the empire were regularly inspected. Here an official procession is greeted with drums and fanfares.

Bronze grave figure, Norway

8 Mesopotamia and Persia are ruled by the Romans under Trajan, but Hadrian soon establishes Roman frontier at the Euphrates river and makes a treaty with the Parthian rulers of Persia and Central Asia.

Gilt-bronze leopard from China

Statue of Buddha, India

10 China is united into an empire in the 3rd century BC; a strong central government is set up, administered by a vast civil service. Silk is traded with the West. Pottery begins to take the place of bronze.

Pharos lighthouse, Alexandria

9 India, largely unified under the Mauryan dynasty between 324 and 187 BC, is now dominated by the Kushans who have close trading links with Rome.

Roman aqueduct, Spain

Emperor Trajan

Roman Tower of the Winds, Athens

Ivory carving from Palmyra, Syria

North African mosaic

7 Rome The Roman empire reaches its greatest extent under Trajan, but already some of its chief problems are becoming obvious – among them the question of who should succeed as emperor, and the poverty of Italy.

The Empire Outside Europe

In Anatolia, in the Near East, and in Egypt, civilization had existed for anything from 1000 to 2500 years before the Romans came. Through the ages the peoples there had become used to being ruled by great empires, and in many ways were far more civilized than the Romans. They were prosperous and there were many centres of learning. When Rome took control of these areas, it did not try to impose its own way of life on them. Instead it was a matter of carrying on, and growing rich from, an ancient pattern of trade, city life, craftsmanship, and agriculture.

The ruins of Palmyra, in Syria. Under the Romans, it became a very important city. In the late 3rd century AD its queen, Zenobia, declared her country independent; she was captured in 272 by the Roman Emperor Aurelian and the city was destroyed in 273.

MAJOR EMPERORS	
27BC–AD14	Augustus
14–37	Tiberius
37–41	Caius (Caligula)
41–54	Claudius
54–68	Nero
69	Year of the Four Emperors
69–79	Vespasian
79–81	Titus
98–117	Trajan
117–138	Hadrian
161–180	Marcus Aurelius
284–305	Diocletian
306–337	Constantine I

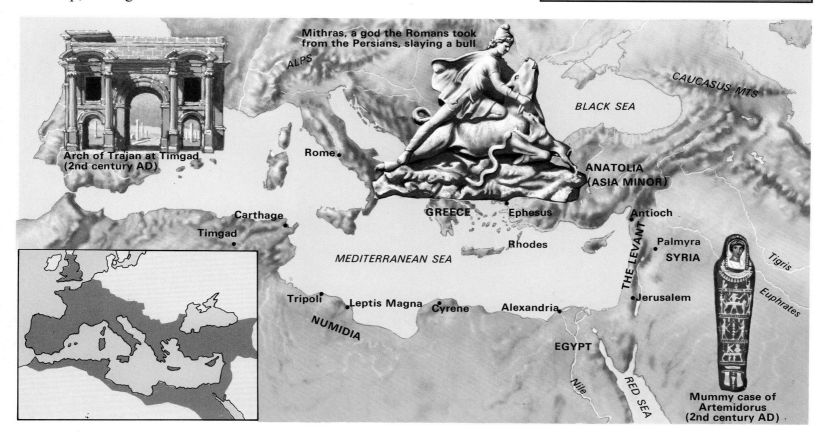

Arch of Trajan at Timgad (2nd century AD)

Mithras, a god the Romans took from the Persians, slaying a bull

Mummy case of Artemidorus (2nd century AD)

Rome's Empire in the East

Rome gained its first overseas territories by defeating Carthage and taking over its colonies. This made Rome a power to be reckoned with. At this time the eastern Mediterranean was dominated by powerful rival kingdoms ruled by Greek kings. These were the descendants of Alexander's generals who had carved up his empire between them. The kingdoms constantly fought with one another to win new territory. Rome, the great new Mediterranean power, seemed to be a useful ally in the struggle for power.

At different times Rome was called in to deal with the ambitious rulers of Macedonia and Syria, who were threatening the kingdoms of Rhodes and Pergamum. At first, Rome fought simply to keep the balance of powers in the east – and for the rich rewards in loot. But there was so much trouble that the Romans lost patience and took control of the whole area. Finally, in 30 BC, the Romans invaded Egypt, the wealthiest kingdom of all. With this, the Roman conquest of the east was complete.

The Division of the Empire

The Roman empire soon proved too vast to be kept firmly under control. The army was enlarged to deal with the attacks of warlike people beyond the frontiers, but new problems arose when powerful army commanders appointed their own candidates as emperor. Weak emperors, barbarian invasions, and economic crises made the empire almost ungovernable. The emperor Diocletian decided to reorganize it completely. In AD 286 he split the provinces and the army into smaller units, all firmly controlled by his own civil service. He divided the empire itself into West and East, and set up an emperor in Rome to rule the West; he ruled the East and had supreme power overall. The system did not work for very long, but it showed that the wealthy East was now more important. The strongest emperor of the 4th century, Constantine the Great, moved his capital from Rome to Byzantium, which he renamed Constantinople. Even after the weaker West fell to barbarian invasions in 476, the Eastern empire remained strong for several more centuries.

AFRICA

Roman rule in Africa stretched all along the Mediterranean coast, and inland until mountains or desert formed a natural barrier. Under the Romans, North Africa became very rich. Miles and miles of irrigation pipes were laid to carry water to farms where grain, vines, and olives were grown. Old cities like the Phoenician Carthage and the Greek Cyrene flourished, and new cities like Timgad in Algeria were magnificent. North Africa has never been so prosperous, for since the Romans were defeated in Africa by the Vandals in the 5th century AD the desert has spread into the fertile areas.

Egypt was a special case. It had far more in common with the long-established cities of Anatolia than with the rest of Africa. It was also specially important for its grain, which brought great wealth to Rome.

The Romans' engineering skills brought more wealth to the cities of Africa and the Near East. Emperors made grants towards building essential but expensive constructions, such as the aqueduct below. Aqueducts carried water over long distances to supply cities and irrigate fields.

The problems of administering the empire led the Emperor Diocletian to divide it into two units, West and East. He proposed a rule of four – two emperors ('augusti'), with two lieutenants ('caesari') who would succeed them after 20 years. This statue shows the four rulers clasping each other in friendship.

The Barbarians

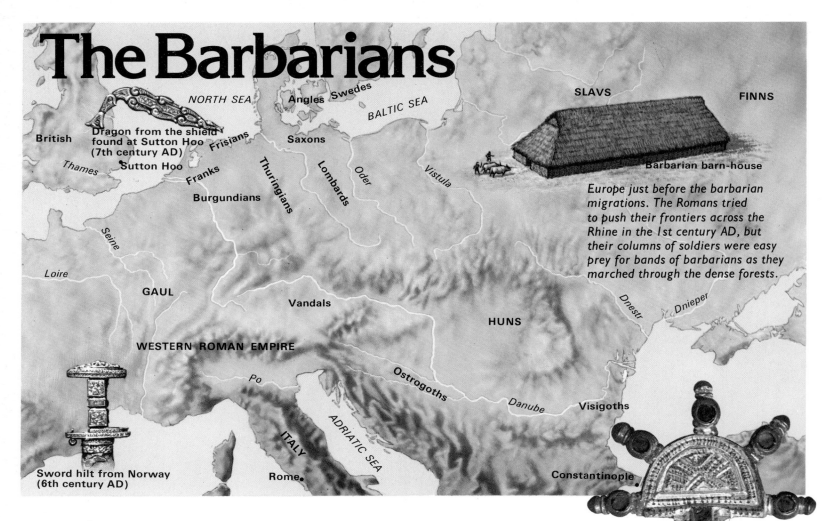

NORTH SEA

Dragon from the shield found at Sutton Hoo (7th century AD)

British

Thames

Sutton Hoo

Frisians

Franks

GAUL

Seine

Loire

Burgundians

Thuringians

Angles Swedes

BALTIC SEA

Saxons

Lombards

Oder

Vistula

SLAVS

FINNS

Barbarian barn-house

Europe just before the barbarian migrations. The Romans tried to push their frontiers across the Rhine in the 1st century AD, but their columns of soldiers were easy prey for bands of barbarians as they marched through the dense forests.

Vandals

WESTERN ROMAN EMPIRE

Po

Sword hilt from Norway (6th century AD)

ITALY

Rome

ADRIATIC SEA

HUNS

Ostrogoths

Danube

Dnestr

Dnieper

Visigoths

Constantinople

The Roman empire in Europe reached east and north to the rivers Rhine and Danube. Within the empire, the Celtic peoples soon took up Roman ways. But across the long frontiers, in the forests and mountains of central and eastern Europe, lived warlike peoples the Romans called 'barbarians' – from the 'bar-bar' sounds of their languages.

Who were the barbarians? Even today no one knows. According to their traditions, they came originally from Scandinavia and the Baltic lands. They migrated south, settling for a time before moving on to another region. Between the mid-3rd and mid-6th centuries AD they moved around so much that this is called the Age of Migrations.

The Romans scorned the barbarians. However, although they did not live in cities, and had only a simple writing system, they had their own well-organized customs and laws. They were also superb metalworkers, and their minstrels composed long and stirring poems. They were great warriors. They stopped the Roman expansion, and raided and harassed the Roman forts. When tribes became more and more crowded against one another during the Age of Migrations, they eventually broke through the frontiers, and overthrew the empire in the west.

Houses and Farms

The barbarians lived in farming villages. Even after they had invaded the western Roman empire they kept clear of the stone-built towns and cities.

A barbarian village was built of sturdy wooden-framed houses: the walls were a sort of woven matting of brushwood, thickly plastered with clay (called 'wattle and daub'). Inside the house were rows of posts, supporting a thatched roof. A house was divided into two sections, one for the family and one for their livestock – a valuable source of warmth in winter. The largest house in the village belonged to the chief. It was fenced off and surrounded by workshops.

Beyond the village lay fields and pastures. Barbarians kept herds of cattle, for hides, meat and milk. Some tribes kept sheep and goats, while pigs could be left to root for food in the surrounding woods and forests. Livestock was more important than crops – but farmers grew wheat, barley, rye, peas and beans.

Barbarian men fastened their cloaks with brooches like this. It is set with garnets. Such precious objects were made by travelling goldsmiths. Far from being primitive and ignorant, the barbarian peoples produced metalwork of the finest quality.

The Nydam boat, discovered in a peat bog in northern Germany. It is the only surviving example of the type of boat used by the Angles, Saxons, Jutes, and Friesians to cross the North Sea to raid England. It is 21 metres (70 feet) long, and needed 30 oarsmen to propel it. The Viking longships of 400 years later were very similar in design.

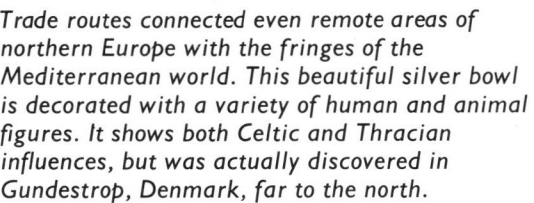

BC	CHRONOLOGY
c200	Peoples living in the Baltic region of northern Europe begin to move south and east, eventually occupying large areas of central and eastern Europe
AD	
c250–550	The Age of Migrations, a confused period of tribal warfare and large-scale movements of peoples
c370	The Huns, fierce nomads from central Asia, drive into south Russia and central Europe; from there Goths and Vandals flee westwards
445	Huns under Attila attack Constantinople. Eastern Roman emperor buys peace. Attila then invades Gaul but is defeated by western emperor. After his death Attila's empire breaks up
476	Rome falls to German tribes. Southern Britain, Gaul, Spain, and North Africa are overrun by barbarian tribes

The Tribal System

Historians group barbarian tribes into 'peoples' like Goths, Vandals, and so on, according to their languages and traditions. But there was no unity about the tribes of any such people. Each tribe was an independent unit which guarded its rights selfishly. Within the tribe was a number of closely knit *kindreds* or family groups.

Tribal affairs were run by an assembly of warriors, and by a council of elders. Chiefs or kings were elected; they had to be skilled war leaders, for the barbarians were ferocious fighters. Many of the poems sung at their feasts were in praise of warriors who had chosen to die rather than retreat.

During the Age of Migrations, the tribal system was weakened as newcomers from the east forced established tribes to leave their lands. In turn these attacked weaker neighbours, or were broken up. Young men grouped together in warbands under a strong leader, who promised treasure in return for loyalty. The rich villas and towns of Roman Gaul were often the targets of warband raids.

The Romans recruited many 'friendly' barbarian bands to fight for them; some chiefs rose to be senior commanders in the Roman army. Towards the end of the empire, barbarians were allowed to settle inside the Roman boundaries. But under weak rulers these people were as hard to control as those beyond the frontiers. One of their commanders, Alaric the Goth, led his people from the lands they had been given down into Italy, to sack Rome itself.

Europe at the time of the fall of Rome, AD 476. Once the barbarians had broken through the frontiers they soon overran Europe and parts of North Africa. The western Roman empire was reduced to a small area of what is now Yugoslavia but 12 years later was taken over by the Ostrogoths.

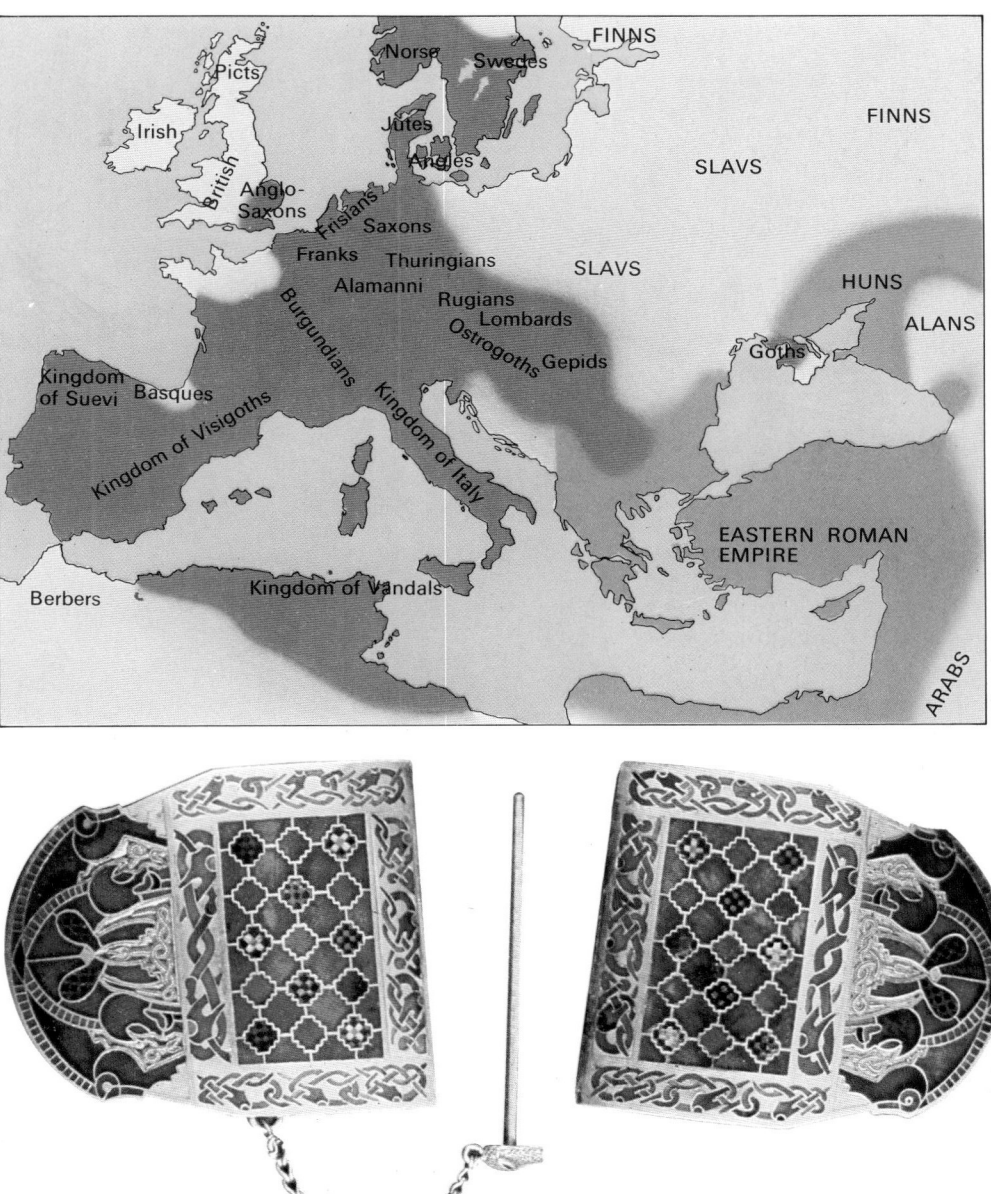

This shoulder clasp is one of a pair found in a ship burial at Sutton Hoo, in eastern England. They date from about 625 AD and the king who wore them owned many beautiful pieces of armour and jewellery. They are finely made and set with garnets and glass in divisions of gold. The 'barbarian' jewellery found at Sutton Hoo is generally thought to be some of the most beautiful and skilfully worked ever found.

The Americas

The first men probably crossed into America around 26,000 BC. At this time there was a land bridge between Asia and Alaska, and it seems likely that hunting Stone-Age people crossed it to become the ancestors of all the Americans. A few sites have been found which show that hunters were living in north Alaska around 24,000 BC and in Mexico in about 22,000 BC. By 10,000 BC the first peoples had reached the tip of South America.

The Americas·were a vast wilderness of forests, deserts, plains, and mountains. Each type of region made different demands on the peoples who lived there. As time went on, each found the best way of adapting to their surroundings. In many areas, groups kept largely to their hunting way of life, adding to their food supply by gathering seeds, nuts, and fruit. They were so successful that this way of life had changed little even by the 19th century AD, long after the Europeans arrived: there was no need for settled farming when it was easy to find food in this way.

Where agriculture developed, as it did before 3000 BC in the Tehuacan Valley in Mexico, three main crops were cultivated: maize, beans, and squashes. Settled villages grew up here around 1500 BC. In other areas, as on the coast of Peru, villages and even towns grew up as far back as 3000 BC. Here there

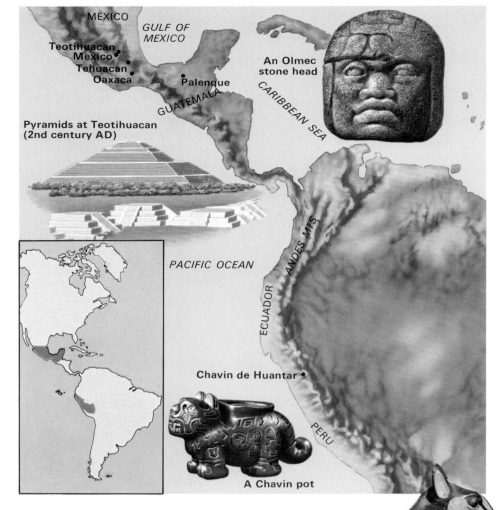

was a good supply of fish and shellfish, but very gradually the people turned to farming. Their crops included the potato and sweet potato, which were first cultivated high in the Andes.

All over the Americas large hunting or agricultural communities grew up. But city-based civilizations developed only in two main regions: Central America, and the north-west coast of South America with the neighbouring Andes mountains.

The Mochica culture of the northern Peruvian coast produced excellent pottery during the first 500 years AD. Pottery was shaped in moulds — the potter's wheel was unknown.

This Olmec pavement is shaped like a jaguar's face. It is nearly 3000 years old but is beautifully preserved since it was covered over by the Olmecs shortly after it was laid. Sometimes the Olmecs showed humans with fangs and claws like a jaguar.

THE OLMECS

The first Central American civilization we know of is that of the Olmecs, which grew up in the swampy tropical forests of the Gulf of Mexico coast around 1300 BC. The main Olmec sites were not cities, but ceremonial centres; they had carefully planned temples, platforms, and courtyards, but few ordinary houses. Farmers lived in the country around, and there were no large towns. Among the most striking Olmec remains are the giant heads carved from huge blocks of rock; the largest stands about 3 metres (10 feet) high. Their heavy features and thick lips are found in other Olmec carvings. Although there are no Olmec centres outside the coast area, Olmec influence stretched far along the trade routes to east and west.

THE MAYA

East of the Olmec area, in another lowland region of tropical forests, grew up the Mayan civilization. Like the Olmec, it had elaborate ceremonial centres but no real cities. Each of four main centres ruled over a quarter of the Mayan region, through a network of lesser centres. Most of the Maya were farmers, living in small villages.

The Maya built tall pyramid temples and beautiful palaces, decorated with stone carvings and wall paintings. They also carved jade, turquoise, and a greenish rock called serpentine. They produced painted pottery and set up vast, curiously carved stone slabs; they were the most skilled astronomers in Central America. The Mayan civilization began around 1000 BC and lasted until about AD 900, when it collapsed. No one knows why. Palaces and villages were abandoned. People either died out or moved away, leaving the jungle to grow over the ruins.

Central America

Central America is the relatively narrow strip of land which joins the great continents of North and South America. It is a region of high volcanic mountains bounded to the east and west by narrow coastal plains. The climate changes with altitude: the hot, wet tropical forests of the plains give way to the cooler, drier mountain uplands and finally the cold, dry regions of the high mountains.

The different civilizations which grew up in Central America had several things in common. They shared many of the same gods and had similar myths; they built stepped pyramids and made human sacrifices. They developed hieroglyphic writing systems and an arithmetic based on 20, and they were skilled astronomers. They worked out a very accurate calendar, with the year divided into 'months' of 20 days; there was a second, sacred cycle of 260 days. Ball courts were important features of every large city; on them a game was played in which heavily padded players tried to propel a solid rubber ball across a central line.

After the Olmec civilization declined, power moved from the lowlands to the highlands of Mexico. Here growing city-states fought for power among themselves. Among these was Teotihuacan, in a side branch of the Valley of Mexico, which by AD 500 had a population of 50,000 and was the most powerful of all the city-states. It had a vast ceremonial section and houses built on a rectangular plan; there were lords and priests, administrators and soldiers. Craftsmen had their own areas according to their trade. Pottery from Teotihuacan was traded over a very wide area, and the influence of its art is seen all over Central America.

CHRONOLOGY

BC	CENTRAL AMERICA	SOUTH AMERICA
5000	Hunting and gathering	Early fishing and farming communities
3000	Beginnings of agriculture; semi-settled communities grow up. First pottery made in Mexico	Pottery is made in Ecuador. Large permanent villages on the coast
2000	Permanent villages are built.	Small-scale irrigation
1000	Early ceremonial centres are built in the Oaxaca region. Olmec civilization in the Gulf Coast	Large ceremonial centres are built 'Cult of the Cat'
AD		
0	Growth of the Maya civilization in Guatemala. Rise of Teotihuacan in Mexico	Mochica and Nazca cultures in coast region
500	Great Maya centres at their height. Teotihuacan also at its greatest	

The palace at Palenque, one of the great centres of the Maya. Centres like this, built in the tropical lowlands of Central America, were complexes of ball courts, temples, and towers.

After 1800 BC, the development of irrigation led to intensive agriculture in Peru. The Peruvians soon learned how to terrace steep mountainsides in order to grow their crops.

South America

The north-western area of South America is very different to Central America. Here the Pacific coast is dry, almost a desert. From it rise the Andes, the second highest mountain range in the world. On the plains, and even in the mountains, irrigation is needed in order to grow crops.

The first civilizations of South America grew up in Peru. Its people developed irrigation systems around 1800 BC and soon large settlements appeared. The steep mountainsides were terraced so that every possible scrap of land could be used. At about the same time pottery began to be made. The first great culture which spread through the region was the Chavin, based on Chavin de Huantar high in the Andes. Here stepped stone platforms, terraces, and sunken courts were decorated with fantastic carvings of man-beasts, often with snarling jaguar-mouths. Sacred images, including jaguars, eagles, and snakes, were also used to decorate pottery, metal-work, and textiles.

Chavin influence lasted from about 1000 to 300. After this there was no one dominant culture, but some six nations have been identified. The best known is the Mochica, on the north coast; its people built temples of mudbrick and huge aqueducts and canals to irrigate their farmland.

The World in AD 500

With the final downfall of the western Roman empire to the invading barbarians, the Mediterranean world is split for good. The west lacks a firm central organization and develops into a number of small-scale national states; they are linked because they are Christian. The eastern half of the empire continues the old pattern of large-scale empire, strengthening its links eastwards, and soon the new religion of Islam spreads through the area. The modern European idea of East and West is taking shape.

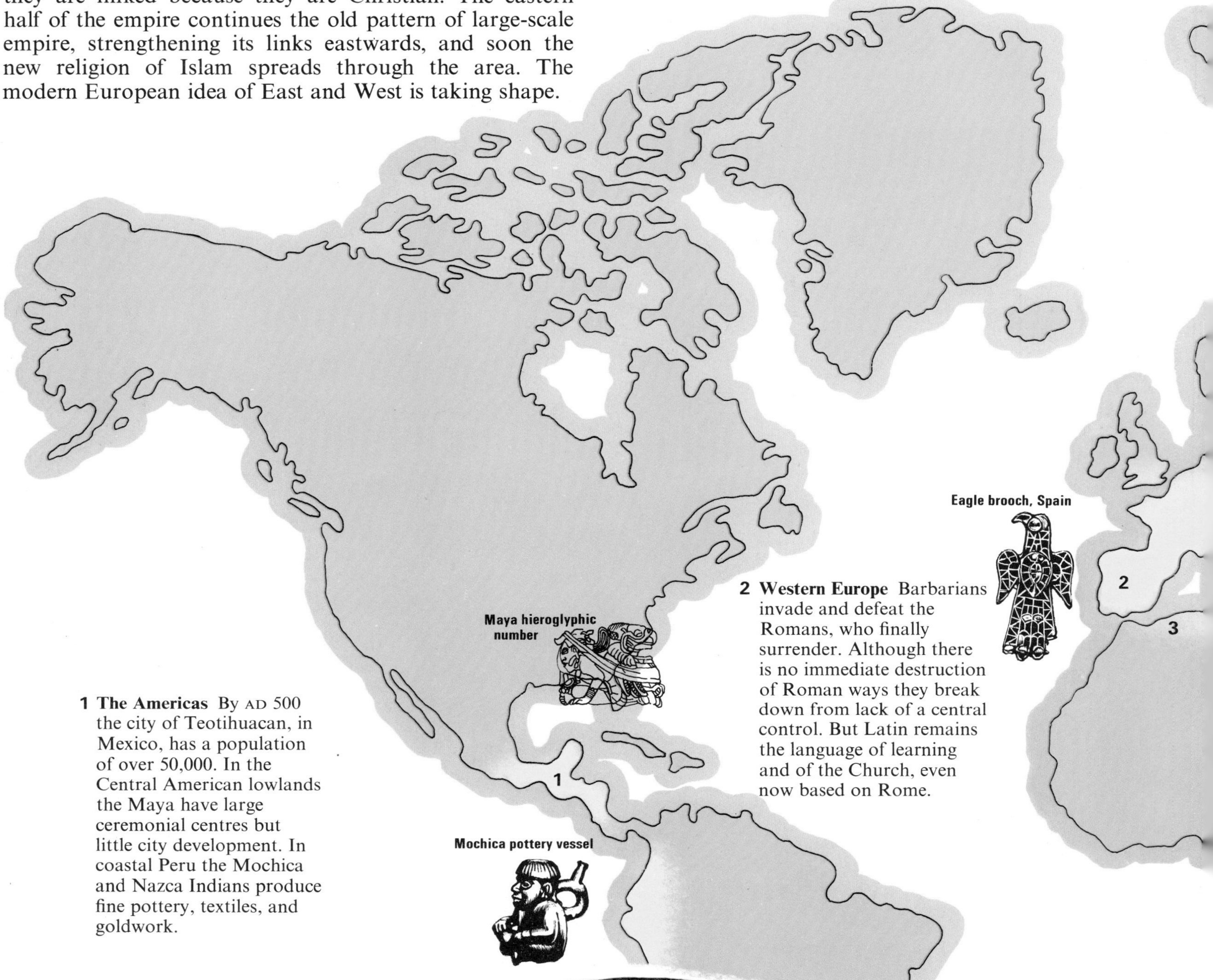

Eagle brooch, Spain

Maya hieroglyphic number

1 The Americas By AD 500 the city of Teotihuacan, in Mexico, has a population of over 50,000. In the Central American lowlands the Maya have large ceremonial centres but little city development. In coastal Peru the Mochica and Nazca Indians produce fine pottery, textiles, and goldwork.

2 Western Europe Barbarians invade and defeat the Romans, who finally surrender. Although there is no immediate destruction of Roman ways they break down from lack of a central control. But Latin remains the language of learning and of the Church, even now based on Rome.

Mochica pottery vessel

A 6th-century mosaic from Ravenna in north-east Italy, showing Christ with St Vitale. Ravenna, a stronghold of the Ostrogoths in the 5th century, was captured by the eastern Roman (Byzantine) empire in the 6th century. In about 750 it passed to the Lombards and later to the Franks.

58

During the 7th century AD the peoples of Arabia were united under a new faith, Islam, founded by the Prophet Muhammad. Between AD 632 and 717 the Muslims, as the followers of Islam are known, gained control of North Africa, Spain, and much of Asia, with the exception of the much-reduced Eastern Roman (Byzantine) empire.

Barbarian glass claw-beaker

Ostrogothic Empress Amalsuntha of Italy

4

Sassanian silver dish, Persia

Bronze Buddha, India

5

Pottery horse from China

6

Pottery figure, Japan

6 China The fall of the Han dynasty in AD 220 is followed by warring states and barbarian invasions in the north. Refugees help to make the south increasingly Chinese in character. In 500 the Tartar emperor in the north forbids the Tartar language and customs; here barbarians, rather than destroying a civilization, have become Chinese themselves. Buddhism is established in the Far East.

4 Eastern Roman Empire After the fall of the West the stronger and richer Eastern empire changes little until the spread of Islam.

5 India The Buddhist kingdoms of north India and Afghanistan are swept away at the end of the 5th century by invading White Huns.

3 North Africa The Roman colonies fall to the invading barbarians; within 200 years the emergence and spread of Islam will link them more strongly with East than West.

Index

Index

Glossary

Administrators Civil servants.
Ally Partner in war or peace.
Alphabetic system Writing system in which a symbol is used for each sound.
Amphitheatre Open-air theatre with rising tiers of seats arranged around a central stage.
Aqueduct Structure for carrying water supply.
Barbarian One living beyond the frontiers of a dominant society.
Bronze Alloy (mixture) of copper and tin.
Ceremonial centre Area designed for religious ceremonies.
Citadel Fortified strongpoint of a city, often on a hill.
City state Area ruled by and for benefit of a city.
Colonize Found settlements abroad.
Culture Skills and way of life of a people or society.

Cuneiform Syllabic writing system formed by wedge shapes, developed in Mesopotamia and widely used in the Near East.
Democracy Rule of society by and for most of the people.
Dynasty Series of rulers from the same family.
Federation States joining together for defence and government.
Feudalism System where a great lord owns the land, which he grants to vassals in return for service, usually military.
Hieroglyphics Writing using picture symbols for ideas or sounds.
Hyksos Egyptian word meaning 'chieftains of foreign countries', used to describe the dynasty of foreign rulers who controlled Egypt in the Second Intermediate Period (1633–1567).
Ingots Metal cast into convenient bars.
Irrigate To supply fields with water.
Jews Name given to those Israelites who returned to Jerusalem and its neighbourhood after the exile to Babylon in the 6th century BC.
Lapis lazuli Semi-precious blue stone used for decoration.
Legends Handed-down religious and historical stories.
Megalithic structures Arrangements of huge stones.

Migrations Movements of peoples.
Nature gods Gods of weather, harvests, places, and so on.
Nomads People who live a wandering life, often in search of grazing for their herds and flocks.
Nuggets Large, naturally occurring pieces of metal.
Oracle bone Piece of inscribed bone used for prophecy in ancient China.
Papyrus Paper made from layers of papyrus reeds.
Parchment Thin piece of goat- or sheepskin used for writing.
Peninsula Piece of land almost surrounded by sea.
Philosophy Study of how to achieve wisdom.
Republic State ruled without a king or dictator.
Seal Carved stone for stamping design to sign or seal documents.
Steppes High cold plains of Russia and Central Asia.
Tableland Raised plain among mountains.
Temple Building used for religious purposes.
Terracotta Shaped and baked clay, often painted and glazed for decoration and to make it waterproof.
Tributary A state which makes payments (tribute) to a more powerful state.
Vassal state A state separate from but ruled by a more powerful one.

ACKNOWLEDGEMENTS

Photographs: Front cover ZEFA; endpapers Michael Holford; title page Josephine Powell; contents page Sonia Halliday (top left), British Museum (centre left), French Tourist Office (top right), British Museum (centre right); page 8 Mark Redknap (top left); 9 Middle East Archives (top left), British Museum (top right), British Tourist Authority (bottom right); 11 Michael Holford; 12 Michael Holford (centre), Ellen Smart (bottom), British Museum (top right); 13 Palace Museum, Taiwan (bottom), ZEFA (top right), Michael Holford (centre); 14 French Tourist Office (top right); 15 Jean Vertut (centre); 16 British Museum; 17 British Museum; 18 Peter Clayton (bottom left); Society for Anglo-Chinese Understanding (top right); British Museum (centre and bottom right); 19 British Museum; 20 Nik Wheeler; 21 British Museum (top left), Musées Nationaux Paris (bottom left), Scala Milan (right); 22 Louvre Paris (centre bottom), Scala Milan (top right), Ronald Sheridan (centre right); 24 Robert Harding Associates (top), Peter Clayton (centre); 25 British Museum (centre), Michael Holford (centre right), Louvre Paris (bottom right); 26 British Museum; 27 Robert Harding Associates; 29 Michael Holford (centre left), Sonia Halliday (centre right), Ekdotike Athens

(bottom); 32 Robert Harding Associates (centre left and right), Air India (bottom); 33 Ellen Smart (top), British Museum (bottom); 35 Ronald Sheridan (centre left), Sonia Halliday (top right); 36 ZEFA; 37 British Museum (top left), Michael Holford (bottom left), Ronald Sheridan (centre right), Sonia Halliday (bottom right); 38 Josephine Powell; 39 Michael Holford; 40 British Museum (bottom left), Louvre Paris (bottom right); 41 Sonia Halliday (top right), Peter Clayton (centre), Musées Nationaux, Paris (bottom); 42 Sonia Halliday; 43 Michael Holford (centre), Sonia Halliday (bottom); 44 Israel Tourist Office; 45 (top and centre) British Museum, Musees Nationaux Paris (bottom); 46 Peter Clayton (centre), William McQuitty (bottom); 47 Society for Anglo-Chinese Understanding (top left and right), Nelson Gallery, Atkins Museum (bottom); 49 ZEFA (top left), British Tourist Authority (centre right); 50 British Museum; 52 Sonia Halliday; 53 Scala Milan; 54 Ashmolean Museum (centre), Schleswig-Holstein Museum (bottom); 55 National Museum Copenhagen (top), British Museum (bottom); 56 Dr W. Bray (bottom left), British Museum (centre right); 57 Michael Holford (centre); Robert Harding Associates (bottom); 58 Sonia Halliday.